NEW YORK SPORTS TRIVIA

IRV FINKEL
DOUGLAS GRUNTHER

Published by Quinlan Press, Inc.
131 Beverly Street
Boston, MA 02114
(617) 227-4870

Library of Congress Catalog Card Number
85-62495
ISBN 0-933341-17-2

First printing October 1985

Cover design by Catherine Silsbee

Photographs pp. 89-97 courtesy of the
National Baseball Library, Cooperstown, NY

We've written this book for two reasons: first, to create an exciting challenge for those of you who are true major leaguers when it comes to sports knowledge; and second, perhaps even more importantly, to provide a dynamic overview of the talent, quirks, and human drama that continuously infuses New York sports. What other city can claim the thrills generated by the Yankees, Mets, Dodgers, baseball Giants, football Giants, Jets, Knicks, Nets, Rangers and Islanders, or the wonderful array of athletes who have graced New York sporting arenas?

We'd like to call special attention to the last two chapters, which include some truly miscellaneous sports nuggets and bridge the gap between the worlds of sports and entertainment. We only hope you have as much fun reading this book as we did putting it together.

Doug Grunther
Irv Finkel

Special thanks to Stephen and Nancy Horn for filling in the gaps, and to Tad Richards for adding spice and a touch of whimsey to a number of chapters.

Table of Contents

QUESTIONS

Baseball

YANKEES

1. In 1976 the Yankees won their first pennant in a dozen years. Who led the Yankee pitching staff in victories that year with 19?

2. Who led the '76 Yanks in home runs with 32?

3. Who led the '77 Yanks in homers with 37?

4. Chris Chambliss hit the pennant-winning home run in 1976, a bottom-of-the-ninth, tie-breaking shot in the fifth play-off game against Kansas City. Who was the winning pitcher for the Yanks in that game?

5. Who served up the home run ball to Chambliss?

6. Which Yankee led the club in batting in the '78 Series with a .438 average?

7. Which Yankee pitcher was credited with two victories in the '77 Series triumph over Los Angeles?

8. What is the significance of the following Yankee scores: 15-3, 13-2, 7-0 and 7-4?

9. In the opening game of the 1977 World Series, the Yankees topped Los Angeles 4-3 in 12 innings. Who got the game-winning hit for New York, his only hit of the Series?

10. Name the Yankee pitcher who won the sixth and final game of the 1978 Series pitching the first complete game of his career.

11. Name all four men who replaced Billy Martin as Yankee manager.

12. What is the record for the highest single-season batting average ever by a Yankee, and who holds it?

13. The most hits by a Yankee in a single season is 231. Who holds that mark?

14. Who is the Yankees' all-time leader in base hits?

15. Who is the Yankees' all-time leader in RBI's?

16. Who is the all-time Yankee leader in losses?

17. Two pitchers compiled win-loss percentages of over .700 while working for the Yanks in over 1,000 innings. Can you name both?

18. Who is the Yankees' all-time leader in shutouts?

19. The Yankees had two 20-game winners in 1978. Who were they?

20. The Yankees had two 20-game winners in 1963. Who were they?

21. The Yankees had two 20-game winners in 1951. Who were they?

22. The Yankees had the only two 20-game winners in the American League in 1937. Who were they?

23. The Yankees had two 20-game winners in 1928. Who were they?

24. What is Tom Zachary's claim to fame?

25. What pitcher, later to toil for the Mets, yielded Roger Maris' 61st homer in 1961?

26. Name the Chicago Cub pitcher on the mound when Babe Ruth hit his "called shot" home run in the 1932 World Series.

27. What is the significance of May 2, 1939, in Yankee history?

28. With what words did Mel Allen greet television viewers of Yankees games?

29. Who was "The Son of the Golden West"?

30. Which Yankee hurled two no-hitters in a single season?

31. Who managed the Yankees to the World Championship in 1947?

32. Who managed the Yankees in 1930, following Miller Huggins and preceding Joe McCarthy?

33. In what season did the Yankees finish tenth?

34. In what season did the Yankees win 110 games, the second-highest total in American League history?

35. From 1926 through 1964, the Yankees finished as low as fourth only once. In what year did the Yanks finish fourth?

36. Which Yankee led the American League in batting in 1945 with a .309 average?

37. Joe DiMaggio led the American League in batting twice, turning the trick in two consecutive years. Which years?

38. How many times did Babe Ruth lead the American League in batting?

39. How many times did Lou Gehrig lead the American League in batting?

40. Which Yankee led the American League in RBI's in 1945 with 111? (He was a first baseman.)

41. Three Yankees have led the American League in RBI's for two consecutive years. Can you name this trio?

42. Which Yankee holds the all-time record for most total bases in a single season?

43. In what two seasons did Mickey Mantle hit over 50 home runs?

44. Who holds the all-time Yankee record for RBI's in a single season?

45. Which Yankee had 19 pinch-hits in the 1953 season?

46. In 1904 a New York pitcher won 41 games. Who was he?

47. Who had the higher lifetime batting average, Lou Gehrig or Joe DiMaggio?

48. Name the pitcher who was twice a 20-game loser with the Red Sox before coming to the Yanks, with whom he won 20 games four times and seven of nine World Series decisions.

49. The 1949 pennant-winning Yankees (Casey Stengel's first Yankee club) had only two players hit 20 or more home runs. Yogi Berra hit exactly 20. Which Yankee led the club with 24 round trippers?

50. Who was the only 20-game winner on the '49 Yanks?

51. Which pitcher led the '49 Yanks with 27 saves?

52. In 1950 the Yanks added a young pitcher to the staff who compiled a 9-1 win-loss record, and a World Series win. Who was this pitcher?

53. What Yankee pitcher of the early 1950s was known as "Plowboy"?

54. Only one Yankee regular hit .300 or better in the 1951 championship year. Can you name this all-purpose player?

55. What veteran pitcher came to the Yanks from the Boston Braves in 1952 and ran up an 11-6 record?

56. This Yankee hurler led the American League in '52 with 160 strikeouts and a 2.06 ERA. Can you name him?

57. In 1953 two Yankee outfielders hit over .300. Mickey Mantle was not one of them. Can you name the two?

58. The '52 Yanks had no 20-game winners, but they did boast a southpaw who led the American League in ERA (2.42) and winning percentage (.800). Who was he?

59. In 1954, among Yankees who batted 300 or more times, this left-fielder compiled the best batting average, with a .319 mark. Can you name this former Washington Senator?

60. Only one Yankee pitcher won 20 in '54, a rookie right-hander. Can you name him?

61. Name the young third baseman who gained a starting spot for the Yanks in 1954, batting .302. (He remained with the club until his 1960 trade to the Kansas City Athletics.)

62. 1955 was the year in which the first black player appeared in a Yankee uniform. Who was he?

63. In 1956 this right-hander won 18 games for the Yanks, and then threw a shutout to win the seventh game of the World Series. Who was he?

64. This right-hander led the Yankee staff in wins in 1957 with 16. He pitched briefly for the Mets in 1964. Name him.

65. Name the little left-hander who came to the Yanks from the Athletics in 1957 and led the staff in ERA with a 2.45 mark.

66. Another player joined the Yanks that year from Kansas City, an outfielder nicknamed "Suitcase." Who was he?

67. Can you guess the three Yankees who tied for the league lead in triples in 1957? Each had nine three-baggers.

68. This Yankee batted .304 in 1958 at the tender age of 42. A former National League great, he joined the Yanks in 1954, went to K.C. the next year, and was back with the Bombers again in '56. Who was he?

69. Name the Yankee hurler who won 21 games in 1958 and was awarded the Cy Young Trophy.

70. Name the Yankee who had a 17-game World Series hitting streak which was stopped in the fourth game of the '58 Series by the Braves' Warren Spahn.

71. Name the spectacled pitcher who came to the Yanks in '58 from K.C. and became the ace of the bullpen for two seasons.

72. The '59 Yankees finished a disastrous third in the American League. Name the two clubs that finished ahead of them.

73. Only one Yank hit .300 or better in '59. That was the first year in which this player got 100 hits for the Yanks, a mark he was to reach for the next seven years consecutively. Can you name him?

74. On what day of the week did Detroit Tiger slugger Charlie Maxwell always murder Yankee pitching?

75. In 1959 the Yanks acquired a third baseman from Kansas City whose erratic fielding earned him the nickname "What a Pair of Hands." He was soon shifted to the outfield. Name him.

76. What Yankee was selected as American League MVP for the 1960 season?

77. Name the right-hander who led the Yankee staff in 1960 with 15 wins. (He started and lost games one and five in the 1960 World Series.)

78. Only one Yankee regular batted over .300 for the 1960 season. He also hit 26 homers. Who was he?

79. Six Yankees hit 20 or more homers in 1961. Name all six.

80. Which Yankee batted .348 in 1961 to lead the team?

81. Whitey Ford won 25 games for the '61 Yanks, but the best ERA among starters was compiled by a young right-hander in his first full big league season. Name this pitcher, who went 14-9 with a 2.68 ERA for the '61 Yanks.

82. Whitey Ford led the American League with a winning percentage of .862 in 1961 (25 wins and Four losses). Another Yankee was second in that category with a percentage of .842. Who was he?

83. Name the rookie starting shortstop for the 1962 Yankees.

84. Name the Detroit Tiger pitcher of the late 1950s and early 1960s who was known as "The Yankee Killer."

85. In 1963 Bill Skowron was traded by the Yankees—to what team?

86. Who replaced Showron as Yankee first baseman?

87. In the four-game Series of 1963, Whitey Ford started twice and Jim Bouton once. Who started the other game for the Yanks?

88. Name the Yankee who Sandy Koufax struck out to end the first game of the '63 Series, thus recording his 15th strikeout of the game and breaking Carl Erskine's record.

89. Name the pitcher who came up to the Yanks in mid-year in 1964 and helped pitch them to the pennant by winning nine of 12 decisions.

90. Three Yankees hit two or more homers in the 1964 Series. Mickey Mantle hit three, and Tom Tresh belted a pair. Which other Yankee hit two homers in that Series?

91. Which Yankee banged out a record-setting 13 hits in the '64 Series?

92. What musical instrument did Phil Linz make famous in August of 1964?

93. In what World Series did Yankee announcer Mel Allen lose his voice?

94. Name the year: The Yanks are battling the Orioles for the pennant. The Birds come to New York for a four game set in mid-September. The Yanks win all four, and close out the season with 11 more wins in a row.

95. Name the year: The Yanks are locked in a three-team race with Baltimore and Chicago. The Bombers drop four straight in Chicago in August, the last games they are scheduled to play against either the Sox or the Birds. In September the Bombers take advantage of the schedule by winning 11 straight against the Angels, A's, Indians and Senators, taking the flag by one game.

96. Name the year: The Yanks are neck-and-neck with the Tigers for the pennant. Detroit comes into the Stadium for a three-game weekend set in early September. The Yanks win all three, then tack on another ten straight wins. Bye, bye, Tigers.

97. Name the year: The Yankees win 103 games under manager Casey Stengel, the only time Casey leads the team over the 100-victory mark.

98. Name the year: The Yanks top the Red Sox in the final two games of the season to edge Boston for the pennant by a single game.

99. Name the season: Things go badly for the Yanks. Babe Ruth and manager Miller Huggins battle, and Ruth is fined $5,000 and suspended. The Yanks finish in seventh place.

100. Yankee Stadium opened in time for what season?

101. Who hit the first Stadium homer on opening day?

102. When was Old-Timers Day at Yankee Stadium instituted on an annual basis?

103. What is the name of the award given to the outstanding Yankee rookie in spring training each year?

104. Who had the first pinch-hit homer in World Series history?

105. The Yankees have played against eight National League teams in World Series competition. Only one of those teams has managed to compile a .500 mark against the Bombers, in terms of total games played. Which team is it?

106. Only one National League team has the edge over the Yanks as far as World Series results are concerned, topping New York on three occasions while losing the title to the Bombers twice. Name the team.

11

107. Who were the Yankees' co-owners during the Stengel years?

108. What year did the Yankees play in their first World Series?

109. What year did the Yankees win their first World Series?

110. Everyone remembers Don Larsen's perfect game in the 1956 World Series. Most everyone knows about Floyd Bevens near no-hitter against the Dodgers in 1947. What Yankee pitcher hurled no-hit ball for 7 1/3 innings against the Pirates in the 1927 Series?

111. Speaking of Beven's near no-hitter, Cookie Lavagetto had the Dodgers only hit, a ninth-inning double that not only spoiled the no-hitter but also won the game for Brooklyn. For whom was Cookie pinch-hitting?

112. Name the veteran right-hander who came to the Yankees late in the 1964 season and helped them to the pennant with fine work out of the bullpen. (He arrived too late in the year to be eligible to play in the World Series.)

113. From 1927 through 1953 the Yankees appeared in 16 World Series, winning 15 of them. Name the only team to stop the Bronx Bombers' string of October triumphs and the year.

114. Twice the Yanks have won back-to-back four-game sweeps in Series play. Can you give both sets of years and the teams the Yanks swept?

115.   In the four years from 1955 through
        1958 the Yankees captured four straight
        American League pennants, despite on-
        ly once having a pitcher win 20 games.
        Name the Yankee 20-game winner of
        that period.

Name the following Yankees:

116.   "The Chairman of the Board"

117.   "Poosh 'Em Up"

118.   "Hug"

119.   "The Major"

120.   "Flash"

121.   "Jumping Joe"

122.   "The Crow"

123.   "Home Run"

124.   "Snake"

125.   "The Naugatuck Nugget"

126.   "Superchief"

127.   "The Springfield Rifle"

128.   "The Knight of Kennett Square"

129.   "Fordham Johnny"

130.   "Sub"

131.   "Steady Eddie"

13

132. "Sarge"

133. "Catfish"

134. "Happy Jack"

135. "Twinkletoes"

136. "Scooter"

137. "Bullet Bob"

138. "Moose"

139. "Prince Hall"

140. October 14, 1976. The Yankees gain a World Series berth for the first time in 12 years when Chris Chambliss homers in the bottom of the ninth to defeat Kansas City. Who was the Yankee winning pitcher?

141. On December 7, 1973, the Yankees traded reliever Lindy McDaniel. They received pitcher Ken Wright, plus what other player?

142. Which three players did the Yankees receive on December 11, 1975, in exchange for pitcher George "Doc" Medich?

143. In exchange for Rusty Torres, Charlie Spikes, John Ellis and Jerry Kenney, the Yankees received two players. One was Jerry Moses. Who was the other player?

144. On June 15, 1976, the Yankees acquired Ken Holtzman, Doyle Alexander, Grant Jackson and Elrod Hendricks from Baltimore. The Yankees sent five players to the Orioles. Rudy May and Dave Pagan were two. Name the other three.

METS

145. Who led the 1962 expansion Mets in homers with 34?

146. Who was second in homers on that team with 16?

147. Which '62 Met led the club with 32 errors, accumulated at a variety of positions?

148. How many consecutive games did the '62 Mets lose at the start of the season?

149. Name the only '62 Met to hit over .300.

150. Which '62 Met had an 0-12 record until he finally won a game in Chicago on the final weekend of the season?

151. The Mets had two pitchers in '62 with the same first and last names. Who were they?

152. The '62 Mets had a team batting average of .240, committed 210 errors, and had a team ERA of 5.04. Within five, how many games out of first place did the Mets finish?

153. Who led the Met pitching staff in shutouts in 1962?

154. In 1963 the Mets had a pitcher who posted a very respectable 3.10 ERA. Can you name this ex-Milwaukee Brave?

155. Which Met hit the ninth-inning Polo Grounds home run to break Roger Craig's endless 1963 losing streak?

156. Ron Hunt finished second in the voting for Rookie-of-the-Year in 1963. Who nosed out of the Met second-sacker?

157. Do you remember the name of the young Met starting shortstop in 1963? He was tabbed as a player for the future, but batted only .193 in 119 games, played only 16 games the following year, and then was gone from the major leagues forever.

158. This Met outfielder came to the team in 1963 after brief stints with the White Sox and the Senators. He created a brief sensation with some timely long-ball hitting, but finished the year with only five homers and a .226 batting average. He never again played big league ball. His name is not unlike another, better known Met outfielder. Can you name him?

159. This young Met southpaw threw a shutout in his first start in 1963. His arm went bad after the season, and he finished his big-league career with a 1-1 record and a 2.72 ERA in 20 innings of work. Can you name him?

160. Which pitcher on the 1962 Mets compiled an 0-4 record with an ERA of 7.71, and was nicknamed "Roadblock"?

161. This outfielder hit over .300 for the Cubs in 1961 and again in 1962, with a total of 49 homers. He went to the Cardinals in '63 but slumped to a .274 average. He came to the Mets in '64, hoping to regain his batting form and supply some left-handed power. Instead, he hit .230 with nine homers in his only Met season. Who was he?

162. This catcher, who played briefly with the Yankees in 1960 and 1961, came to the Mets in '63 and batted .302 in 42 games for New York. He hit .270 the following year, but was noted more for his absence of catching skills than for his batting. Can you name him?

163. Can you name the third baseman who led the '64 Mets in homers with 20 after being acquired early in the season from the White Sox? (He later played for the Yankees.)

164. Two Met regulars hit .300 or better in 1964. One was Ron Hunt (.303). Who was the other?

165. Can you name the Met catcher who hit .311 in 1964, coming to bat officially only 164 times? Most of his 51 base hits (41 singles, 10 doubles, no triples or homers) seemed to be perfectly placed bloopers or bleeders. His lifetime major league average was .235, though he played in the big leagues for all or part of 13 seasons.

166. Name the veteran shortshop who starred for the Mets in '64, '65 and part of '66.

167. The '64 Mets had three pitchers who won in double figures. Al Jackson led the staff with 11 wins. Can you name the two right handers who each won ten?

168. In what year did Wes Westrum take over the managerial reins from Casey Stengel?

169. Which Hall-of-Fame southpaw came to the Mets in 1965 and compiled a 4-12 record?

170. This young right-hander threw a shutout for the Mets in 1964 for his first big-league win. It was his only victory of the year (he finished 1-5). He won 11 for the Mets in 1966 before being traded to Pittsburgh. Who was he?

171. This 6'7" right hander threw a shutout for the Mets in 1965, his only win of the year (he compiled a 1-10 mark), and the second and final win of his major league career. Can you name this lanky ex-Met?

172. The '65 Mets may not have had very good pitchers, but they had big pitchers. Can you name the 6'6", 220-pound right-hander who won six and lost six for the Mets that season? He was with Houston the following year, but never figured in another major league pitching decision. (He was 0-1 with the Mets in '64, and wound up with a lifetime mark of 6-7.)

173. The Mets acquired a young outfielder from the Cardinals for the '65 season. Strong, fast, 6'1" and 190 pounds, he was touted as a potential superstar. He hit .245 with 15 homers for the Mets in '65, then batted .193 the next year and .118 in limited action in '67. Who was he?

174. In what year did the Mets escape the National League cellar for the first time?

175. Name the first team to finish behind the Mets.

176. The '66 Mets had a former National League MVP at third base. He hit .266 with 14 homers for the Mets, his only full season with the club. Who was he?

177. The '66 Mets had two starters with winning records. One was a native New Yorker who came to the Mets from the Giants. He pitched for the White Sox in the 1959 World Series, having won 18 and lost six that year. He was 11-10 for the Mets in '66. Who was he?

178. In 1967 the Mets fell back into the cellar, despite the batting of this native of Brooklyn who came to the Mets from the Dodgers and hit .302 with a team high 16 homers. Who was he?

179. The '67 Mets boasted the National League's Rookie-of-the-Year. Name him.

180. Which Met rookie compiled a 19-2 record with a 2.08 ERA in 1968?

181. The Mets acquired an outfielder from the White Sox in 1968. In his first Met season he hit .217 with five homers. Who was he?

182. Name the two Mets who batted .300 or better in the miracle year of 1969.

183. Name the Met second baseman who clubbed two homers as the Mets swept three straight from Atlanta in the National League Championship Series.

184. This Met pitcher worked seven strong innings in relief to win the final game against the Braves and send the Mets on to the World Series. Who was this pitcher?

185. How many games did the Mets need to win the 1969 World Series against the Baltimore Orioles?

186. Who led the Mets in the Series with three wins?

187. Who led the Mets in batting in the Series with a .455 average?

188. Which pitcher recorded the first Met World Series win ever?

189. Which pitcher recorded the final out in the first Met Series victory and got the save?

190. What pitcher started the third game of the '69 Series for the Mets?

191. Whose bunt was misplayed by the Orioles Pete Reichert, allowing the win-

ning run to score in the fourth game of the Series?

192. Which Met pitcher knocked in a pair of runs in the '69 Series?

193. The Mets had one stolen base in the '69 Series. Who stole it?

194. In the 1973 National League Championship Series, the Mets had three homers, all by the same player. Who was it?

195. Who yielded the home run to Pete Rose in the 12th inning of game four of the '73 play-offs to absorb the loss?

196. Who pitched the only shutout for the Mets against the Reds in that play-off Series?

197. Name the Met southpaw who started from the fourth game of the '73 play-offs. (He was 12-3 that season for New York.)

198. The Mets had four homers in the '73 World Series, two of them by one player. Who hit the two homers?

199. Which two Met pitchers threw a combined three-hit shutout against the A's in game five of the Series?

200. Name the only pitcher on the 1962 Mets with a winning record.

201. Who was the only ten-game winner on the '62 Met pitching staff?

202. What pitcher won the first Met game ever?

203. Who was the only Met in 1962 to bat over .300?

204. Name the first Met ever elected to a starting position on the National League All-Star team.

205. On Father's Day in 1964, Jim Bunning of the Philadephia Phillies pitched a perfect game against the Mets at Shea. Name the Met who struck out to end the game.

206. Who replaced Wes Westrum as manager of the Mets for the final 11 games of the 1967 season?

207. How many regular season games did the champion '69 Mets win?

208. Which Met regulars hit .300 or better in 1973?

209. In the '69 Series Tom Seaver and Jerry Koosman each started two games for the Mets. Name the other Met starter in their five-game triumph over the Orioles.

210. Aside from the three starters, only three other men took the mound for the Mets in the '69 Series. Can you name them?

211. In the 1973 National League Championship Series win over the Cincinnati Reds, this Met led the team with three home runs despite batting only .200 Name him.

212. The first Met line-up, on April 11, 1962, featured a catcher who never hit more than five homers in any of his 14 major league seasons. Who caught that first Met game?

213. Three of the starting Met infielders that night were ex-Dodgers. Name them.

214. Who was the starting shortstop for the Mets in their first game?

215. Who was the Mets' first starting pitcher?

216. Whom did the Mets play in their first National League game?

217. Who had the first Met hit?

218. Who had the first Met homer?

219. Which Met hit his 100th career home run in 1963 and celebrated by backpeddling around the bases?

220. What team did the Mets play in their first home game at the Polo Grounds on April 13, 1962?

221. What team did the Mets play in their first home game at Shea Stadium on April 17, 1964?

222. The 1962 Mets lost the season series with all but one National League team. With which team did the '62 Mets manage a 9-9 split?

223. In the championship year of 1969, the Mets won their season series with all but

two National League teams. They split with Cincinnati 6-6. Which team took the season series from the Mets in '69?

224. The Mets achieved particular success in '69 against one National League club, taking 11 of the 12 games played. Which team served as the Mets' patsies in their championship season?

225. In 1970 Tom Seaver fanned 19 Padres in one game. How did Seaver conclude his great performance?

226. Who was Jimmy Qualls?

227. Name the four players the Mets received from Cincinnati in exchange for Tom Seaver.

228. What player came to the Mets in exchange for Nolan Ryan, Leroy Stanton, Don Rose and Francisco Estrada?

229. Who did the Mets give up to get third baseman Joe Foy?

230. Name either of the two players the Mets received from Minnesota in exchange for Jerry Koosman.

231. Name the two players the Mets received from Texas in exchange for Lee Mazzilli.

232. The Mets won the 1973 National League pennant without having a 20-game winner on their pitching staff. Four Mets won ten or more games. Tom Seaver, Jerry Koosman and Jon Matlack were three of them. Name the fourth.

233. Who led the 1973 pennant Mets in homers with 23?

DODGERS

234. In 1941 the Dodgers won their first pennant in 21 years. Who led the team and the league with 34 home runs?

235. Name the Dodger great who led the National League in batting in 1941.

236. The '41 Dodgers had two 22-game winners. Name both.

237. Name the ex-"Gas House Gang" star who played left-field for the '41 Dodgers.

238. In 1942 the Dodgers won 104 games, but finished in second place. Which team won the pennant that year?

239. Can you name the outfielder who led the 1943 Dodgers in home runs with the grand total of nine?

240. The 1944 Dodgers tumbled to seventh place in the National League. On that team was a rookie right-hander whose given name (in full) was Calvin Coolidge Julius Caesar Tuskahoma. Years later he won 19 games in one season for Cleveland. What was his last name?

241. The '44 Dodgers boasted the league's leading batter, with a .357 average. Who was it?

242. In 1945 the Dodgers finished third, led by a right-handed pitcher who won 18

games. It was the only time in his career that this hurler won ten or more games. Who was he?

243. What do the Dodger teams of 1946, 1951 and 1962 all have in common?

244. Name the two Dodgers who tied for the team lead in homers in '47.

245. Name the right-hander who won 21 games for the pennant-winning '47 Dodgers.

246. Dixie Walker played right field for the '47 Dodgers, and Pete Reiser played left. Who played center for the Bums?

247. Name the Dodger reliever who led the National League in saves in 1947.

248. Who replaced Leo Durocher as Dodger manager during the 1948 season?

249. This Dodger rookie of 1948 was nicknamed "Shotgun." Who was he?

250. The two leading pitchers on the Dodger staff in 1948 both had last names beginning with the letter 'B'. One was Ralph Branca. Who was the other?

251. The 1949 pennant-winning Dodgers had five pitchers win ten or more games. Three of them were Don Newcombe, Preacher Roe and Ralph Branca. Name the other two.

252. In 1950 the Dodgers lost the pennant to the Phillies on the final day of the

season. Name the Dodger who was thrown out trying to score with the potential game-winning run in that climactic contest.

253. This rookie went 15-4 for the Dodgers in 1952, with a 2.15 ERA. Who was he?

254. Carl Erskine led the Dodger staff in wins in 1953 with 20. Next on the squad was a pitcher acquired that year from the Phillies, who won 15 and lost only five for the Brooks. Can you name him?

255. Name the Dodger who led the National League in batting in 1953 with a .344 average.

256. Billy Bruton of the Braves led the National League in stolen bases in '53 with 26 thefts. The next four highest stolen-base totals were all posted by Dodgers. Name all four.

257. Name the pitcher who led the '54 Dodgers in saves with 24. (He pitched for Brooklyn from 1952 until early in the '56 season, winning 14 games while losing ten.)

258. Name the two rookie pitchers who won 13 and lost only four between them for the Dodgers in their championship year of 1955.

259. In the 1955 Series, among Dodgers with ten or more at-bats, who led the team in batting with a .333 average?

260. Which Dodger belted four homers in the '55 Series?

27

261. Johnny Podres won two games in the '55 Series, including the seventh. What two pitchers recorded the other Dodger wins?

262. Name the former Chicago Cub who played infield for the Dodgers in '56 and '57 and was nicknamed "Handsome."

263. Which two Dodger pitchers threw no-hitters during the 1956 season?

264. Which Dodger led the National League in saves in 1956 with 19?

265. Only one Dodger regular hit .300 in 1956, and he hit that figure exactly. Who was it?

266. 1957 was the final year for the Dodgers in Brooklyn. In what place did the Bums finish?

267. Name the player who replaced Pee Wee Reese as the Dodgers starting shortshop in 1957.

268. The '57 Dodgers boasted two pitchers with the lowest ERA's in the National League. Who were they?

269. What beer sponsored Dodger games on radio and television in the 1950s?

270. Who emceed the Dodger pre- and post-game TV shows?

271. What clown performed at Dodger games during the 1957 season?

272. What TV channel carried the Dodger games?

273. Name the only Brooklyn Dodger who led the National League in batting for two consecutive years.

274. Which Dodger set a club record by grounding into 27 double plays in 1956?

275. Name the two Dodger 20-game winners in 1951.

276. Throughout the 1930s, only two Dodger pitchers recorded 20-win seasons. One did it in 1932, the other in 1939. Can you name both?

277. Name the 20-game winner for the pennant-winning Dodgers of 1920.

278. Which Dodger pitcher led the National League in strikeouts for seven consecutive seasons?

279. Which Dodger pitcher with a lyrical name led the National League in strikeouts in 1936, while winning 18 games and losing 19?

280. Name the Dodger pitcher who posted an .889 winning percentage in 1940, a National League mark that lasted until Pittsburgh's Elroy Face went 18-1 in 1959 for a .947 percentage.

281. Which Brooklyn Dodger first baseman led the club in RBI's five consecutive years?

282. Which Dodger first baseman led the club in RBI's three straight years in the early 1920s?

283. Who played first base for the 1947 National League Champion Dodgers?

284. In 1953 the Dodgers had three players each of whom batted over .300, belted over 30 homers, and drove in over 100 runs. Name this trio.

285. The Dodgers first series appearance came in 1916. They lost the series 4 games to 1, dropping game 2 in 14 innings by a 2-1 score. Name the team they played.

Give the nicknames of the following players:

286. Carl Furillo

287. Wilbert Robinson

288. Pete Reiser

289. Pee Wee Reese

290. Otto Miller

291. August 31, 1950. Gil Hodges makes history. What does he do?

292. What were the famous words spoken by Father Herbert Richmond?

293. By what two other names have the Dodgers been known during their 20th century Brooklyn history?

294. Who replaced Wilbert Robinson as Dodger manager?

295. Who managed the Dodgers from 1934 to 1936?

296. The only All-Star Game ever played in Ebbets Field was the 1949 Classic. Name the Dodger pitcher who took the loss in the 11-7 slugfest.

297. Who asked the question: "Is Brooklyn still in the league"?

298. Name the man who joined the Dodgers in 1938 as executive vice-president. (He brought lights to Ebbets Field, as well as people like Leo Durocher, Dolf Camilli, Dixie Walker and Joe Medwick.)

299. In what year was Dodger manager Leo Durocher suspended for the season for "conduct detrimental to baseball"?

300. What did Leo Durocher do in 1948 that was so unusual?

301. Who was the last Dodger manager to direct the team wearing street clothes?

302. What did Dodger pitcher Leon Cardore do on May 1, 1920, that earned him a place in the record-books?

303. Who hit the only Dodger home run during the seven-game 1947 Series?

304. Who hit the only Dodger home run during the 1941 Series?

31

305. Jack Coombs was the first Dodger pitcher ever to accomplish what significant feat?

306. The Dodgers lost 2-1 in 14 innings in the second game of the 1916 World Series. Name the pitcher who went the distance to beat Brooklyn.

GIANTS

307. What do Willie Mays, Bill Terry and Larry Doyle have in common?

308. Name the New York Giant who led the National League in RBI's in 1942 and 1947. (He also led the league in that category in 1940 while playing for another team.)

309. The last New York Giant to lead the National League in RBI's turned the trick during the 1951 season. Who was he?

310. Name the Giant who was selected as MVP twice during the 1930s.

311. Which Giant holds the club single-season record for winning percentage by a pitcher with an .833 mark?

312. Name the Giant outfielder who struck out only seven times in 1956 in 453 official at-bats.

313. The Giant record for total bases in a single season was also set in 1930. By whom?

314. The last Giant pitcher to lead the National League in strikeouts turned the trick in 1944. Who was he?

315. Name the last Giant 20-game winner.

316. The Giants won the pennant in 1937 with two 20-game winners. Carl Hubbell was one. The other was a rookie who never again won more than 14 in any one season. Can you name him?

317. Hubbell won 21 games for the Giants in 1934. Who led the team with 23 wins?

318. In 1903 Christy Mathewson won 30 games for the Giants. The next year he won 33, but he did not lead the club in victories either time. Who did?

319. In what year did Mathewson win 37 games?

320. Name the 20-game winner for the champion Giants of 1921.

321. In 1954 the champion Giants had two pitchers tie for the league lead in winning percentage with .750 marks. Name them.

322. Name this pitcher: He led the National League twice in a row in winning percentage, going 17-7 in 1927 for a .708 mark and 25-9 the following year for .735. He came to the Giants early in the '27 season from the Braves, and was sent on to the Reds early in 1930.

323. Which two Giants with sound-alike last names led the club in RBI's in 1949 and 1950, respectively?

324. Which shortstop holds the Giant record for home runs in a single season with 23?

325. Name the all-time great Giant shortstop who knocked in 101 runs in 1934, a team record for that position.

326. Name the Giant (a former Cardinal backstop) who set team records for most homers and most RBI's by a catcher in 1947 with 35 round-trippers and 122 RBI's.

327. The catcher mentioned above did not lead the Giants that year in home runs or RBI's. Who did?

328. The 1947 Giants poled a record breaking 221 home runs. Bobby Thompson hit 29 homers. Name the other Giant outfielder of 1947 who blasted 36 homers.

329. The second baseman on the '47 Giants hit 17 homers, and later became Giant manager. Name him.

330. This Giant outfielder played for John McGraw from 1911 through 1921. He is the all-time Giant leader in stolen bases with 334, two more than Willie Mays. His name is the same as a famous comedian. Who is he?

331. In which of the following categories does Mel Ott lead Willie Mays on the all-time Giant list: runs scored, doubles, total bases or RBI's?

332. Why did it take the 1921 Giants eight games to defeat the Yankees (playing in their first World Series)?

333. Name the Giants' pitcher who hurled three shutouts in a single World Series.

334. In which three consecutive years did the Giants lose the World Series?

335. The 1951 National League champion Giants boasted two 23-game winners. Name them.

336. Who was the only 20-game winner for the champion Giants of 1954?

337. Name the New York Giant outfielder who batted .417 with two home runs against the Yankees in the 1923 Series. (Hint: He became a famous manager.)

Name the following Giants:

338. "The Barber"

339. "The Brat"

340. "Goofy"

341. On July 2, 1933, the Giants swept both ends of a remarkable doubleheader from the Cardinals. They won the opener 1-0 in 18 innings. Who pitched the complete game shutout?

342. The Giants won the nightcap, also 1-0, topping the Cards' young ace, Dizzy Dean. The winning Giant pitcher was nicknamed "Tarzan." Who was he?

343. Who resigned on June 3, 1932?

344. Following the 1926 season, long-time Giant favorite Frankie Frisch was traded. What great second-sacker came to New York in that deal?

345. What Giant pitcher was called "The $11,000 Lemon"?

346. What Giant pitcher won 19 straight decisions?

347. September 23, 1908. Who neglected to touch second base?

348. October 16, 1912. Game seven of the World Series. The Giants score a run in the top of the tenth to take a 2-1 lead over the Red Sox. Who dropped a routine fly ball to open the bottom of the tenth, opening the gates for a pair of Red Sox runs and costing the Giants the Series?

349. Who was the Giant pitcher when Snodgrass muffed the fly ball?

350. October 20, 1924. Game seven of the World Series the Giants and the Washington Senators are tied 3-3 in the bottom of the 12th. A grounder to third takes a bad hop and goes over the head of the Giants' 18-year-old rookie third-sacker. The Senators score the winning run on the play. Name the unfortunate Giant infielder.

351. Name the Giant outfielder who was banned from baseball for life because he offered a $500 bribe to Phillies shortstop Heinie Sand to throw a game.

352. What Giant coach was also implicated and banned from baseball? (He had played for the Yankees briefly in 1911 and 1912.)

353. What did Carl Hubbell do between July 17, 1936, and May 27, 1937?

354. Who was known as "Little Napoleon"?

355. This Giant hit .458 in the 1951 Series (11 for 24). Name him.

Give the nicknames for the following Giants:

356. George Kelly

357. Alvin Dark

358. Hal Schumacher

359. Ross Youngs

360. Bobby Thompson

361. Bill Rigney

362. Joe Moore

MISCELLANEOUS

363. Name the five Hall-of-Famers Carl Hubbell fanned in succession in the 1934 All-Star Game at the Polo Grounds.

364. Four National Leaguers hit homers in that Yankee Stadium game. One had a brother on the Yanks, and the other three all had last names with the same letter. Can you name them all?

365. The Brooklyn Dodgers won only one World Series, in 1955. The Dodgers won the final game 2-0. Which Dodger drove home both runs?

366. Which Yankee made the final out of that game?

367. How was the final out recorded?

368. In the legendary fourth game of the 1947 World Series, when Yankee Bill Bevens came within one out of throwing a no-hitter against the Dodgers, who wound up as the Dodger winning pitcher?

369. Cookie Lavagetto ripped the dramatic double to break up the no-hitter and win the game for the Dodgers. Name the Dodger runners who scored on Lavagetto's hit.

370. Both Dodgers who scored were in the game as pinch-runners. For whom were they running?

371. How did the tying run get to second base for the Dodgers?

372. How did the eventual winning run reach base?

373. Don Larsen's Perfect Game: Which game of the 1956 Series was it?

374. Who was the home plate umpire?

375. Who was called out on strikes to end the game?

376. Who homered for the Yanks to break a scoreless tie?

377. Which New York team had players named Joe Moock and Lute Barnes?

378. Name the National League team which beat the Mets 32 out of 36 times during the first two Met seasons ('62 and '63, while the Mets played home games at the Polo Grounds.)

379. October 3, 1951. The Giants and the Dodgers meet in game three of the National League play-off to decide the pennant. Who was the Giants' starting pitcher?

380. Who was the Dodgers' starting pitcher?

381. Which Giant pitcher got credit for the win?

382. What was the score of the game going into the bottom of the ninth?

383. Who led off the Giant ninth with an infield single?

384. Don Mueller, second Giant batter in the ninth, singled. What was noteworthy about that hit?

385. The third Giant batter of the inning popped out. Who was he?

386. Which Giant delivered a run-scoring double, putting the tying run at second and driving Newcombe from the game?

387. Mueller was injured sliding into third on the two-base hit. Who pinch-ran for Mueller?

388. What was the count on Bobby Thompson when he hit the "shot heard 'round the world" off Ralph Branca?

389. Who jumped on manager Leo Durocher's back in the third base coach's box following Thompson's homer?

390. Who was the Dodger catcher for the climactic 1951 game?

391. Who was the on-deck batter when Thompson homered?

392. For which New York team did Noodles Hahn and Bubbles Hargrave play?

393. For which New York team did Sweetbreads Bailey and Boom-Boom Beck pitch?

394. For which team were Slim Salle, Ferdie Schupp, and Rube Benton the World Series starting pitching rotation?

395. The first two World Series games ever played between the Yankees and Giants resulted in shutout victories for the upstart American Leaguers. Name the two Yankee hurlers who blanked McGraw's team.

396. Despite the two Yankee shutout victories to open the Series, the Giants won the initial World Series meeting of

the two teams five games to three. Which Giant pitched a four-hit shutout to win the final game?

397.   The first two World Series games ever played in Yankee Stadium were both decided by one run margins. In both games, a home run by the same player proved the margin of difference. Name the outfielder who hit the first two World Series homers at Yankee Stadium.

398.   Name this player, who later managed the Yankees: In 1924 he hit two World Series homers against the New York Giants. Both games in which he homered ended with 4-3 scores, and both times the Giants lost.

399.   Who won 20 or more games in a season more times, Larry Jansen or Carl Erskine?

400.   Who won 20 or more games in a season more times, Don Newcombe or Whitey Ford?

401.   Name the first non-Yankee to win the Babe Ruth Award.

402.   Name the first non-New Yorker to win the Babe Ruth Award.

403.   Which of the following had a 200-hit season: Pete Reiser, Bobby Richardson or Mel Ott?

404.   In which Subway Series was there a tie game?

Football

GIANTS

1. Who is nicknamed "The Bald Eagle"?

2. Who is nicknamed "Chuckin' Charlie"?

3. Who is nicknamed "Big Red"?

4. In what season did Y.A. Tittle establish an NFL record with 36 touchdown passes? (The record has since been broken.)

5. Name the Giant who booted 126 consecutive points after touchdown between 1958 and 1961.

6. Name the Giant who led the NFL in punting in 1957.

7. During the Giants' last-place 1964 campaign, this part-time quarterback threw only three interceptions in 143 pass attempts. Name this Ivy League graduate.

8. In 1966 these two Giants hooked up on a 98-yard touchdown pass play, the longest in Giant history. Name the quarterback and the receiver.

9. What Giant intercepted 79 passes in his career, establishing an NFL record?

10. Name the Giant who returned kick-offs for 987 yards during the 1964 season, the third highest NFL total up to that time.

11. What Giant ran an interception back for a 102-yard touchdown against Dallas in 1961?

12. What Giant ran an interception back for a 101-yard touchdown against the Rams in 1966?

13. In what department did the Giants' Howard Livingston lead the NFL in 1944?

14. In what department did the Giants' Francis Reagan and Otto Schnellbacher both lead the NFL?

15. Which Giant tied for the league lead in interceptions in 1963, after leading the league in that category two years earlier?

16. Which Giant led the NFC in pass receptions in 1971?

17. Name the Giant quarterback who led the NFL in passing as a rookie in 1933.

18. Name the Giant quarterback who led the NFL in passing in 1935 and again in 1938.

19. What Giant led the NFL in rushing as a rookie in 1936 with 830 yards gained?

20. Name the Giant who led the league in rushing in 1943 and 1944.

21. What Giant was the NFL's rushing leader in 1950 with 971 yards gained?

22. This Giant led the NFL in field goals made in 1938 (five), 1939 (seven) and 1943 (three). Who is he?

23. What year was Y.A. Tittle named co-winner with Jim Brown of the Jim Thorpe Award as the NFL's Most Valuable Player?

24. Which Giant led the NFL in scoring in 1963?

25. Who was the first Giant receiver to top 1,000 yards in a season?

26. Which Giant runner set an NFL record (since broken) by rushing for 218 yards in a game against the Chicago Cardinals in 1950?

27. Name the first Giant runner to top the 1,000-yard mark in single season rushing.

28. In what year did Giant end Bob Schnelker catch nine passes in a championship game?

29. Gene Roberts, a back for the Giants in the late '40s, was known by what nickname?

30. Name the Giant tackle of the late '40s and early '50s who earned acclaim in

later years as a football broadcast analyst.

31. What end out of Columbia played for the Giants in '48, '49 and '50?

32. From what team did the Giants acquire Arnie Weinmeister in 1950?

33. Name the two great backs who joined the Giants as rookies in 1951 and 1952, respectively.

34. Steve Owen became the Giants' head coach in 1931. What season was Owen's last with the club?

35. In 1953 the Giants acquired a young center from Northwestern. Who was he?

36. In 1953 the Giants also gained a tackle from Morgan State. What was his name?

37. From which team did the Giants obtain Andy Robustelli?

38. Who replaced Roosevelt Grier in the Giants' defensive line in 1963?

39. In the mid-'50s the Giants carried three quarterbacks. One was Charlie Conerly. Name the other two.

40. The 1956 champion Giants had two linebackers, both of whose last names began with the letters 'Sv.' Name both.

41. What famous event took place at the Polo Grounds on December 9, 1934?

42. Name the former New York University great who starred in the Giant backfield in the preceding game.

43. Who was the head coach of the 1956 NFL championship Giants?

44. In the 1958 championship game against the Baltimore Colts, two Giants scored touchdowns. Name the scorers.

45. In 1960, why were the Dallas Cowboys happy that the Giants were in the league?

46. Who was the offensive coach for the 1958 Giants?

47. Who was the defensive coach for the 1958 Giants?

48. The Giants won the Eastern Division title in 1958, 1959, 1961, 1962, and 1963. What team usurped the crown in 1960?

49. In the final game of the regular season, the Giants played a 7-7 tie with the Browns, thereby winning the Conference title by half a game. Cleveland's Ray Renfro dropped a sure touchdown pass in the game's closing moments, preserving the tie. What year did this occur?

50. In what year did the Browns top the Giants 8-3 in a Conference play-off game? (The Giants had defeated the Browns twice in regular season games.)

51. In what year did the Giants beat Cleveland three straight times to win the Conference title?

52. In what year did the Giants lose to the Chicago Bears 23-21 in the first NFL championship game?

53. In what year did the Giants win the NFL championship for the first time?

54. In what year did the Giants compile a 9-1-1 regular season record, the best in the league? (They allowed only 85 points all season, also a league best, then were drubbed 27-0 by Green Bay in the championship game.)

55. In what year did the Giants finish in a tie for first in the Eastern Division with the Redskins, but lose the play-off 28-0?

56. In what year did the Giants finish first in the East with an 8-1-1 mark, the best in the league? (They allowed only 75 points all season, by far the lowest total in the league, but again lost to Green Bay in the title game, this time 14-7.)

57. The Giants fell from first place in the East one year all the way to last place the next—twice. In what years?

58. In what year did the Giants compile a dismal 1-12-1 record, permitting 501 points to be scored against them?

59. In what year did the Giants beat the Steelers 33-17 in the final game of the regular season to win the Conference ti-

tle? (Hint: Frank Gifford's one-handed catch of a third-down pass was the key play.)

60. In what year did the Giants score 41 points in a game against the Redskins, yet still lose the game by a whopping 31-point margin?

61. This Football Hall-of-Famer played tackle-end for the Giants in 1927-28 and 1936. He was also named to the Baseball Hall of Fame as an umpire. Name him.

62. This Giant holds the dubious record for most passes intercepted in one championship game (six in 1946). He was suspended indefinitely afterward for involvement in fixing the game. Name him.

63. This Giant Hall-of-Famer was center-linebacker from 1931 to 1945. He never missed a game in 15 years. Name him.

64. The founder of the Giants was named to the Hall of Fame in 1963. Who was he?

65. For what college did Phil Simms play?

66. In 1961 the rookie head coach of the Giants was named NFL Coach of the Year. Name him.

67. This TV sports commentator played defensive end in college, but became a field goal kicker for the Giants from 1958-1961. Name him.

68. Who was the first tight end to lead the NFL in receiving?

69. This Hall-of-Famer played tackle for the Giants from 1926-1931. As Giants head coach, he holds the record for coaching the most championship games (eight). Who is he?

70. This one-time Giant went on to become the first black coach in the NFL. He was also the first black player elected to the Hall of Fame. Name him.

71. What does The 'Y.A.' in Y.A. Tittle stand for?

72. Who was the Giants' first head coach (in 1925)?

73. On December, 28, 1958 the Baltimore Colts defeated the Giants 23-17 in what has been called "the greatest game in the history of professional football." What was the special significance of the game's ending?

74. "Red" Simpson, a Giant linebacker (1948-1950), is credited as being the first in pro football to do what?

75. In 1960 Frank Gifford was knocked unconscious and did not play the rest of the season after being tackled by which Philadelphia linebacker?

76. This former Olympic decathalon gold medalist was a member of the Giant squad when the NFL came to New York in 1925. Name him.

77. The last 0-0 tie in the NFL was in 1943. What teams played in that game?

78. Which 1964 Olympic gold medal sprinter was signed by the Giants?

79. Name the former Giant soccer-style place kicker who first played for Buffalo.

80. Giant executive Jim Trimple advanced the game of football with what innovation?

81. Which New York Giant star of the '70s and '80s is a cousin of baseball great Carlton Fisk?

82. In his rookie season (1983) Ali Haji-Sheikh set an NFL record for most field goals. Did he boot a) 33, b) 35 or c) 38?

83. In their first 1984 play-off game, the Giants topped the Los Angeles Rams 16-13. Who scored the only Giant touchdown?

84. At which college did Harry Carson play football?

85. Name the Giants' head coach who compiled a win-loss record of 7-28.

86. Who holds the Giant record for most field goals in a single game (with six)?

87. Which of the following was **not** a Giants first-round draft choice during the 1970s?
    a) Jim Files
    b) John Hicks
    c) Earnest Gray

88. True or False: The Giants have won only once on "Monday Night Football" (through 1984).

89. Against what team did the Giants play their first regular season overtime game, and what was the result?

90. The last time the Giants had the number-one pick in the NFL draft, they selected a running back out of Auburn. Name him.

91. Name the last Giant (through 1984) to amass 1,000 or more yards as a pass catcher in a single season.

92. What college did Leonard Marshall attend?

93. What college did Jerome Sally attend?

94. In the 1980s the Giants have one first-round draft pick out of Michigan and another from Michigan State. Name both.

95. In their play-off-bound 1984 season, only once did the Giants score 30 or more points. Against which team did they pile on the points?

JETS

96. The New York Jets played in the first ever "Monday Night Football" game on ABC-TV. What team was the Jets' opponent in that 1970 game?

97. Who won the game?

98. The original name of the Jets was the New York Titans. Who was the team's first owner?

99. Who was the first head coach?

100. Who was the starting quarterback for the team in its first season (1960)?

101. What was the team's win-loss record in 1960? (It posted an identical mark in 1961.)

102. In what year did the team acquire the nickname 'Jets'?

103. In what year did the Jets first post a win-loss percentage of better than .500?

104. Name the linebacker from Ole Miss who starred for the New York American Football League team in the early 1960s.

105. In what year did Weeb Ewbank become head coach of the Jets?

106. Name the Clemson University runningback who was a Jet workhorse in the early and mid '60s.

107. What was linebacker Ed McDaniel's nickname?

108. What Princeton runningback joined the Jets in 1965?

109. What defensive standout joined the Jets in 1964 after playing college ball in Buffalo?

110. Which Jet intercepted two passes in the team's Super Bowl triumph over the Baltimore Colts?

111. Which team ended the Jets' chances of repeating as NFL champs with a play-off win over New York in 1969?

112. In 1972 Joe Namath passed for over 400 yards in two games. Against which teams did Namath have his big days?

113. In 1960 two New York pass catchers topped the 1,000-yard mark for the season. Name them.

114. Name the Titan who accumulated over 2,000 yards in combined net offense (rushing, pass receiving, punt and kickoff returns) in the 1962 season.

115. Which Jet led the AFC in scoring in 1972?

116. Who was the first Titan or Jet to lead the AFL in pass receptions, and in what year did he do it?

117. Name the Titan who led the AFL in interceptions in 1962.

118. Which Jet led the AFL in interceptions in 1964?

119. This 300-pound offensive tackle out of Maryland State came to the Jets in 1963, and later helped protect young Joe Namath. Name him.

120. After the 1964 college season, the Jets signed two hot-shot quarterbacks. One was Namath. Who was the other?

121. What team did the Jets defeat in the 1968 American Football League championship game?

122. Everybody remembers the great upset the Jets scored in Superbowl III over the heavily favored Baltimore Colts. Do you remember the final score of that game?

123. What college did Jets great Mark Gastineau attend?

124. The longest punt on record, 98 yards, was kicked by a Jet on September 21, 1969. Name him.

125. By what name do we now know Jet defensive tackle Larry Foulk?

126. This Jet holds the record for most pass receptions in a Super Bowl game (eight received, 133 yards), yet he didn't score a touchdown in that game. Name this Joe Namath target.

127. Who was the head coach of the 1969 championship Jets?

128. In the 1968 season this Jet field goal kicker kicked a record-breaking 34 field goals. Name him.

129. On November 17, 1968, the Jets and the Oakland Raiders played a game forever to be known as "The Heidi Bowl." What was the score when the

game went off the air, and what was the final score?

130. Who scored the only Jet touchdown in Super Bowl III?

131. In April, 1981, which Jet married the daughter of Hall of Famer Jim Brown?

132. In 1965, Joe Namath's pro-rookie season, he threw 18 touchdown passes. Who caught 14 of those 18 passes?

133. What ex-Jet running back once sported a Mohawk haircut?

134. Which of the following was not a first-round draft pick of the Jets?
    a) Burgess Owens
    b) Wesley Walker
    c) Marty Lyons
    d) John Riggins

135. What player from Notre Dame was drafted by the Jets in the first round of the 1982 draft?

136. Name the Jet first-round draft choice who played for Jackson State and was an outstanding pass receiver.

137. In 1976 Lou Holtz resigned as Jets coach after 13 games. Who coached the Jets in the final game of the '76 season?

138. In 1975 Charley Winner was released after nine games had been played. Who coached the Jets for the remainder of the '75 season?

139. What college did Joe Klecko attend?

140. The Jets lost their first seven games on "Monday Night Football." They finally won in 1979. What team did they defeat?

141. How many times have the Jets had the top pick in the NFL draft?

142. Freeman McNeil went over the 1,000-yard mark in rushing in 1984. Prior to that, who was the last Jet runner to accomplish this feat?

143. Name the only Jet ever to lead the NFL in rushing.

144. Through 1984, what distinction do the Jets share with the Pittsburgh Steelers, the Green Bay Packers and the San Francisco 49ers?

145. Through 1984, there are three NFC teams with the Jets have never defeated. Can you name them?

146. The Jet record for pass receptions in a single game is 17. Who holds that mark?

147. Who was the Jet leader in pass receptions for the 1984 season?

COLUMBIA

148. In what year did Columbia win its one and only Ivy League football championship?

149. Which team tied Columbia for the title that year?

150. Name the only Ivy League team to defeat Columbia in that championship season.

151. Who was the starting quarterback on the Lions' Ivy League championship team?

152. Who coached that team?

153. Name the starting halfback on Columbia's 1922 football team. (Hint: He's best known for another sport.)

154. Name the captain of Columbia's only league championship football team, who became head coach in later years.

155. In what year did Columbia register a magnificent upset of the undefeated Army team?

156. Who threw the winning touchdown pass for Columbia in that game?

157. Who made the catch in the end zone for the Lions?

158. By what score did Columbia defeat Army?

159. To which school did **The Columbia Daily Spectator** refer when it wrote, "Win or lose, it is an equal disgrace to play them. The linking of the two names detracts as much from our prestige as it adds to their reputation. . . . The Columbia man knows that there is no friendship, no rivalry, no comparison of any nature between ourselves and _____"?

160.   What song was written by Roy Webb,
       Morris Watkins and Corey Ford?

Basketball

KNICKS

1. The Knicks won their first NBA title in 1970. What players made up the starting lineup in the final game against L.A.?

2. What former Knick also played pro baseball with the Chicago White Sox?

3. Former Knick Jerry Lucas started a business after his basketball days ended based on an unusual talent. What was it?

4. Who did the Knicks trade to Baltimore in order to get Earl Monroe?

5. What was the name of the trainer for the 1970 championship Knicks?

6. On November 18, 1972, the Knicks scored an impressive win, coming back from an 18-point deficit in under six minutes. Who were they playing?

7. Who holds the Knick all-time record for points in one game? How many points?

8.   Who previously held that record?

9.   Who was the Knicks' first round draft pick in 1979?

10. What Knick player, besides Bernard King, went to college at the U. of Tennessee?

11. After Willis Reed retired in 1974, who was the starting center?

12. Who is the all-time assist leader on the Knicks?

13. For what high school did Albert and Bernard King play?

14. Where did former Knick Coach Red Holzman play college ball?

15. Who was head coach of the Knicks before Red Holzman took over in 1967?

16. After Willis Reed played his immortal 27 minutes against the Lakers in the final game of the 1970 playoffs, who replaced him?

17. What two Knicks were nicknamed "Living Legends 1 and 1A"?

18. In 1958-59, the Knicks compiled a 40-32 record, good for second place in the NBA Eastern Division. They made the play-offs for the first time since 1955, and would not appear there again until 1967. Who coached the '59 Knicks?

19. Name the forward from Santa Clara who led the '59 Knicks in scoring.

20. Which team eliminated the '59 Knicks in the play-offs?

21. Which Knick guard of the late '60s went on to play a significant role in the Boston Celtics 1969 championship season?

22. Which former Princeton star who went on to a career as a sportscaster played for the Knicks for three seasons in the late 1940s?

23. This 6'5" player joined the Knicks for the '49-'50 season. He played five years for New York, averaging in double figures four times with a high of 14.9 ppg in '50-'51. He later coached the Knicks. Name him.

24. In '52-'53 the Knicks finished first in the Eastern Division. Which team stopped the Knicks in the play-offs?

25. Name the Knick of the early '50s who starred at Colgate in his college days, and has a son now playing in the NBA.

26. Name the 6'5" Michigan State star who came to the Knicks in 1959 and is known for his jumping ability.

27. This former Minneapolis Laker guard averaged 15.6 ppg for the Knicks in '60-'61. It was his final NBA season. Name him.

28. This 6'10" center led California to the NCAA title in 1959, and to a runner-up

finish in 1960. The Knicks drafted him, but he played only two seasons in New York, barely averaging five ppg. He did stick around the NBA for 12 seasons, scoring over 1,000 points for Philadelphia in '69-'70. Name him.

29. For two seasons in the early '60s the Knick roster featured four players all of whose last names started with the same two letters. Can you name this quartet?

30. This guard twice averaged better than 22 ppg for the Detroit Pistons. He played one season for the Knicks ('62-'63), but is best known as an NBA coach. Name him.

31. A great college star, this 6'6" swingman came to New York after spending his best NBA years with Philadelphia. 1966 marked the end of his career with the Knicks. Name him.

32. This former Celtic (and major league baseball player) spent two seasons with the Knicks in the early '60s. Name him.

33. Two brothers from St. Bonaventure each played one season for the Knicks in the early '60s. Name them.

34. This former Holy Cross star was nicknamed "The Shot." He was high scorer in the 1961 NIT tournament with 120 points in four games. His entire NBA career consisted of 11 games—five with Boston, six with the Knicks—in the '62-'63 season. Name him.

35. This U. of Cincinnati center outplayed Jerry Lucas, leading the Bearcats to their second consecutive NCAA title in 1962. The Knicks had high hopes for him, but his NBA career lasted only 65 games. Name him.

36. This former Wake Forest forward came to New York from Philadelphia early in the '63-'64 season, and led the Knicks in scoring, averaging just over 17 ppg. He played two more seasons for the Knicks, but failed to reach double figures. Name him.

37. Late in the '64-'65 season the Knicks acquired a former NYU All-American from the San Francisco Warriors. He played 19 games as a Knick, averaged 4.4 ppg, and that was the end of his NBA career. Name him.

38. The Knicks had two outstanding rookies in '64-'65. One was Willis Reed. Name the other, a power forward from Texas Western.

39. What Knick guard of the '60s was nicknamed "Butch"?

40. In the Knicks' glorious '69-'70 championship season, the club won its season series from all but two NBA teams. Which teams had the regular season edge on the Knicks?

41. In which of the following categories did the champion '69-'70 Knicks lead the NBA: rebounds, scoring or fewest points allowed?

65

42. Who led the Knicks that year in field goal percentage?

43. Six Knicks averaged in double figures in the title season. Reed, Frazier, Barnett, DeBusschere and Bradley were five. Who was the sixth?

44. Name the former Wichita State center who played back-up to Willis Reed that year.

45. The Knicks won their second NBA championship in 1973, topping the Lakers in how many games?

46. What was the Knicks' final standing for the '72-'73 regular season?

47. In which of the following categories did the '72-'73 Knicks lead the NBA: fewest points allowed, assists or field goal percentage?

48. Who led the '72-'73 Knicks in field goal percentage?

49. Name the former UCLA guard who played as a reserve on the '73 championship Knicks.

50. Name the first coach of the Knickerbockers.

51. From the start of the NBA ('46-'47) until the '69-'70 season when Walt Frazier and Willis Reed made the team, only one Knick was ever selected to the NBA first-team All-Stars. Who was he?

52. On December 6, 1947, this Knick rookie set an NBA record by scoring 47 points in one game. Name him.

53. Who was the first black Knickerbocker?

54. In 1970 the Knicks topped the Los Angeles Lakers in the championship round of the NBA playoffs. What teams did the Knicks defeat in earlier rounds?

55. In 1972 the Knicks reached the NBA finals but lost to the Lakers. Who played center for the Knicks that year?

56. Whom did the Knicks give up to obtain Dave DeBusschere from the Pistons in the '68-'69 season?

57. In 1951 the Knicks reached the NBA finals, lost the first three games, came back to win the next three, but lost heartbreakingly in game seven 79-75. Name the team that topped them.

58. Who was the first Knick Rookie-of-the-Year?

59. What do Bill Hosket, Don May and John Warren have in common?

60. Name the two brothers who played together for the Knicks in the early '50s.

61. Who is nicknamed "Dollar Bill"?

62. Who is nicknamed "Clyde"?

63. Who is nicknamed "The Pearl"?

64. Which Knick scored more points in a single season, Carl Braun or Bill Bradley?

65. Which Knick had more points scored in a single season, Willis Reed or Willie Naulls?

66. Who averaged 20 or more ppg in a season more times, Ken Sears or Dave DeBusschere?

67. Which of the following never averaged 10 ppg or higher in any season with the Knicks: Nat Clifton, Phil Jackson or Dick McGuire?

68. What is the record for most points scored by a single player in one game against the Knicks?

69. The Knicks set a record of sorts by making two trades with the same team, in the same year, for players with virtually the same last name. Who were they?

70. What Knick star of the '50s became a doctor?

71. What was Willis Reed's number?

What are the nicknames of the following Knicks?

72. Harry Gallatin

73. Howard Komives

74. Tom Washington

75. Nate Bowman

What are the alma maters of the following Knicks?

76. Don May

77. Mike Riordan

78. Dave Stallworth

79. Walt Frazier

80. Dick Barnett

81. John Warren

82. Nate Bowman

83. Phil Jackson

84. Willis Reed

85. Bill Hosket

86. Dave DeBusschere

87. Bill Bradley

88. Cazzie Russell

NETS

89. What was the Nets' first home court?

90. From whom did the Nets get Rick Barry?

91. Why did Rick Barry leave the Nets?

92. What Net was nicknamed "The Whopper"?

69

93. What Knick star became general manager of the Nets?

94. What was George Carter's claim to fame with the Nets?

95. Where did Dr. J. play college ball?

96. What year did the Nets enter the NBA?

97. Who was responsible for selling Dr. J. to Philadelphia?

98. What was the sale price?

99. Who was the first ex-Knick to play for the Nets?

100. What Net player has a brother who stars for the Knicks?

101. What two Net players (one present, one past) were at one time the starting backcourt for the Knicks?

102. Why did the Nets pay the Knicks $4 million dollars in 1977?

103. Who coached the Nets' 1974 championship team?

104. Who was chief assistant?

105. Where did the Nets play in New Jersey before they moved to the Meadowlands?

106. What Net player's father was coach of the team?

107. Who else came to the Nets in the deal that brought them Julius Erving?

108. What Net star became assistant general manager of the club?

109. The Nets, when they joined the NBA, used a promotional slogan advertising a team-up of stars that never actually happened. What was it?

110. What Net star claims to come from the planet "Lovetron"?

111. Name the Net player, later killed in a tragic accident, who was the subject of a sexy beefcake poster.

112. Who was the first coach of the Nets?

113. Who was the Nets' first leading scorer?

Hockey

RANGERS

1. The National Hockey League was organized in 1917. The first New York team appeared in 1925. What was the team's name?

2. Who led the New York team in scoring in the '25-'26 season?

3. The New York Rangers joined the NHL for the '26-'27 season. What two other teams joined the league at the same time?

4. In what place in the American Division did the Rangers finish their first season?

5. How many Stanley Cup championships have the Rangers won?

6. What is the last year in which the Rangers won the Stanley Cup?

7. Whom did they defeat in the final round?

8. How many games did the finals go?

9. Who was the coach of the last Ranger team to win the Cup?

10. In what other years did the Rangers win the Cup?

11. Who coached the other Stanley Cup champion Ranger teams?

12. How many times have the Rangers won the final Cup game in New York?

13. Which Ranger won the Hart Trophy (MVP) for the '58-'59 season?

14. Which Ranger won the Hart Trophy for the '49-'50 season?

15. Which Ranger was MVP for '47-'48?

16. Which Ranger won the Lady Byng Trophy, for "sportsmanship and gentlemanly conduct combined with a high standard of playing ability," seven times?

17. Name the Ranger who won the Lady Byng Trophy in 1950.

18. Two different Rangers won the Lady Byng in 1957 and 1958. Name both.

19. Which Ranger won the 1972 Lady Byng?

20. In 1970-'71, Eddie Giacomin of the Rangers shared the Vezina Trophy with a teammate. Name "Fast Eddie's" mate.

21. That Ranger Vezina win was the first in over 30 years. Who had won the one and only previous Ranger Vezina?

22. What other New York goalie won the Vezina?

23. The Calder Trophy is awarded to the top NHL rookie. What New York player won the award in 1935?

24. Name the Ranger Calder Trophy winner of 1942.

25. Rangers won the top rookie award in consecutive years, 1953 and 1954. Name these two Ranger favorites.

26. Who was the Ranger Calder winner in 1973?

27. Who was the first Ranger to win the Norris Trophy as the NHL's outstanding defenseman?

28. What Ranger won the Norris Trophy just prior to Bobby Orr's domination of that honor?

29. Which NHL trophy did Ranger Pentti Lund win?

30. Who coached the Rangers during the 1960-'61 season?

31. Who was the player coach of the Rangers in '61-'62?

32. What former Ranger took over as coach during the '62-'63 season, and was eventually replaced by Emile Francis?

33. Who was the Rangers' first coach?

34. Official NHL All-Star teams have been selected since the '30-'31 season. Which Ranger right wing made first team All-Stars that year?

35. Name the Ranger All-Star defenseman of the '34-'35 season who played most of his career with the Black Hawks.

36. Two players with sound-alike last names tied for first team All-Star at right wing for the '37-'38 season. One was a Ranger, the other a Toronto Maple Leaf. Can you name them?

37. Which position did Bryan Hextall play?

38. Until 1956, the Rangers went 13 consecutive seasons without a first team All-Star. Which Ranger broke the spell?

39. In 1951-'52 this Ranger led the team in scoring, finishing fourth in the NHL with 61 points. Who is he?

40. This player led the Rangers in goals scored in his first three seasons with a total of 83, but netted only 31 more goals in his abbreviated career. Name him.

41. Name the player who came to the Rangers from Toronto for the '54-'55 season and led the club with 29 goals, tying Gordie Howe for the fifth best total in the NHL that year.

42. Who was the Rangers back-up goalie in the late 1950s and early '60s?

43. Who led the 1940 Rangers in scoring with 24 goals and 39 points?

44. The Rangers finished atop the NHL regular season standings in 1942. Who led the club (and the league) in goals scored with 32?

45. This Ranger led the club in scoring for eight straight seasons from '56-'63, before he was traded to Toronto midway through the '63-'64 campaign. Name him.

46. Playing with the Rangers, this rugged defenseman made NHL first team All-Stars three times and second team once in the four seasons from 1956 through 1959. Name him.

47. Name the long-time NHL defensive great who came to the Rangers in 1961 and won the '61-'62 James Norris Trophy as the league's top defenseman.

48. Name the oft-maligned Ranger defenseman who won the Norris Trophy for the '66-'67 season. (He scored 12 goals that season, the only time in his long career he scored more than seven times.)

49. Who is nicknamed "The Eel"?

50. Who is nicknamed "The Chief"?

51. By what nicknames were the following Rangers better known: Lorne Worsley, Emil Francis, Lou Fontinato and Donald Raleigh?

52. What part-Indian Ranger defenseman was nicknamed "The Chief"?

53. Who is the only Ranger to have had his number retired?

54. What was the Rangers' last Stanley Cup championship year?

55. Who was their coach that year?

56. How was Walter Tkaczuk's name correctly pronounced? How was it thought to be pronounced for his first few years on the Rangers?

57. What great Montreal defenseman of the 1950s became a player-coach of the Rangers?

58. Who were "The GAG-line"?

59. What did "GAG" mean?

60. Who was the first native New Yorker to play for the Rangers?

61. What normally career-ending injury did Rod Gilbert come back from twice?

62. What one-time Ranger goalie was the first man to wear a mask in an NHL game?

63. Who was the last Ranger goalie not to wear a mask in a game?

64. Who did the Rangers give up in the trade for Phil Esposito?

65. Who else did they get besides Esposito?

66. Why was Ranger announcer Bill Chadwick called "The Big Whistle"?

67. For what quote will Allan Cohen, the Madison Square Corporation's vice president in charge of the Rangers, live in infamy?

68. What Ranger retired the Lady Byng Trophy for sportsmanship after winning it seven consecutive years?

69. What dubious honor has been won by Rangers Lou Fontinato, Vic Hadfield and Reggie Fleming?

70. What chant did Ranger fans of the '50s use to greet NHL senior referee Red Storey every time he skated out onto the ice?

71. In 1977, the Rangers drafted Lucien DeBlois and Ron Duguay, overlooking what future mega-star?

72. Who replaced Emil Francis as Ranger coach/general manager in 1976?

73. Where did the Rangers get Anders Hedberg and Ulf Nielsen?

74. Who had been their linemate on that team?

75. What former Ranger is married to superstar model Carol Alt?

76. From where did Herb Brooks come to the Rangers?

77. What former Ranger became a trainer and driver of harness racers?

78. Whose Ranger career scoring record did Rod Gilbert break?

79. The last time a Ranger won the Art Ross Trophy was in 1942. Who won it?

80. The 1950-'51 Rangers needed help, so a famous New York restauranteur concocted a brew which changed their losing ways. Who invented the "Magic Elixir"?

81. In 1971 the Vezina Trophy for outstanding goal tending was shared by which two Rangers?

82. What Ranger was Rookie of the Year for the 1972-'73 season?

83. This goal tender holds the record for career shutouts with 103. He played for the Rangers and four other teams. Name him.

84. In the 1928 Stanley Cup games, the Ranger coach had to play goalie because of an injury to the regular goalie. Name this coach.

85. What is the nickname of former Ranger player and head coach Fred Shero?

86. In the thrilling 3-2 play-off loss to the Islanders, this Ranger led the club in scoring with six points (two goals and four assists). Who is he?

87. What did the Rangers do in the '70-'71, '71-'72, and '72-73 seasons that they have done on no other occasion?

88. The Ranger record for most victories in a single season is: a) 45, b) 49 or c) 52?

89. Can you name four of the players the Rangers sent to Colorado to obtain Barry Beck?

90. Name the Ranger defenseman who joined the club in the '74-'75 season, and had his best offensive year in '80-'81 with 27 goals.

91. What former WHA Rookie-of-the-Year joined the Rangers for the '78-'79 season?

92. Who is older, Dave or Don Maloney?

93. In the '83-'84 season, this Ranger had 19 power-play goals, only one fewer than league leader Wayne Gretzky. Name him.

ISLANDERS

94. Who was the Islanders' first coach?

95. In 1972 the Islanders set a record for fewest victories in a season by an NFL team. How many games did they win?

96. What Olympic star joined the 1979-'80 champion Islanders in the middle of the season?

97. Who was team captain at the start of the '79-'80 championship season?

98. Who was the team captain at the end of the '79-'80 season?

99. Who carried the Cup around the ice for the victory tour?

100. What Islander star threatened to hold out at the beginning of the '79 "season of destiny"?

101. Who scored the overtime goal to win the 1980 Stanley Cup?

102. Who was credited with the assists?

103. What is the name of Bryan Trottier's less successful hockey-playing brother?

104. Which Sutter brothers have played for the Islanders?

105. What ex-Islander players have become announcers for the team?

106. To whom did the Islanders trade Chico Resch?

107. Who paired with Ed Westfall to form the Islanders' classic penalty-killing duo?

108. What team did Al Arbour coach before the Islanders?

109. Who scored the overtime goal to beat the Flyers for the Islanders' first Stanley Cup?

110. The Islanders' first game in the NHL was in October, 1972. Who scored the first Islander goal?

111. Which Islander won the Calder Trophy for Rookie of the Year for the 1973-'74 season?

112. Who was the Islanders' first coach?

113. Who replaced him?

114. Who was the Islanders number one pick in the 1974 draft?

115. Who did the Islanders trade to L.A. for Butch Goring in 1980?

116. What was the nickname give to the starting offensive line of Gilles-Bossy-Trottier?

117. Name the only four original Islanders to play on the first Stanley Cup team.

118. What 19-year-old rookie scored a hat trick in the second game of the 1975-'76 season?

119. Who was the Islanders' number one pick in the 1973 Amateur Draft?

120. An Islander holds the record for quickest overtime goal in history. Who is he?

121. What is the name of Denis Potvin's autobiography?

122. What player did the Islanders acquire from Cleveland in a trade for J.P. Parise and Jean Potvin?

123. What Hicksville park was used as the Islanders training camp?

124. Whom did the Islanders trade to Washington to obtain Gordie Lane?

What are the nicknames for the following Islanders?

125. Coach Al Arbour

126. Duane Sutter

127. Brent Sutter

128. Ken Linseman

129. Bobby Nystrom

130. Dave Langevin

131. Name the former Islander who went on to become the team's TV color man.

Photo

1. What was the address of this Madison Square Garden?

2. What characteristic did this building not have that the subsequent buildings had?

3. When was this Madison Square Garden opened?

4. Who designed the tower?

5. What was the address of this Madison Square Garden?

6. What was the first event held here?

7. When was the present Madison Square Garden opened?

8. What streets bound this Garden?

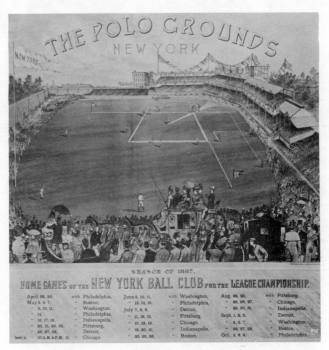

9. What was the first professional baseball park in New York proper?

10. Who opposed the Giants in their first NL game?

11. What was the site of the second Polo Grounds previously called?

12. What separated the Polo Grounds and Yankee Stadium?

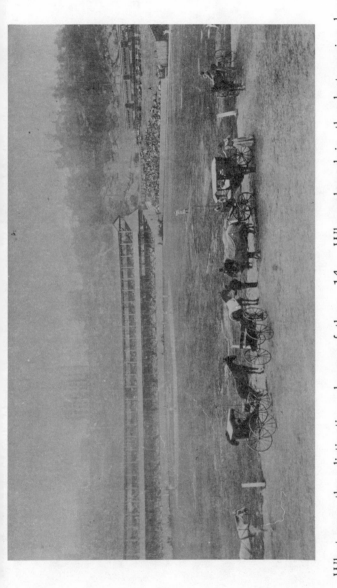

13. What was the distinctive shape of the Polo Grounds?

14. Who played in the last major league game at the Polo Grounds?

15. Where did the Yankees play prior to their own stadium?

16. Who opposed the Yankees in their stadium opener?

18. What Yankees were commemorated by the original center field monuments?

17. What has been the popular nickname for center field at Yankee Stadium?

19. What was previously at the site of Yankee Stadium?

20. What year did the "new" Yankee Stadium open?

21. What four streets bordered this park?   22. When was the last game played at Ebbets Field?

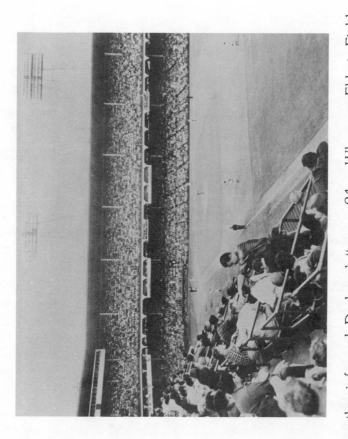

23. What was the informal Dodgers' "or-
chestra" known as?

24. Who was Ebbets Field named after?

25. At its deepest, how far from home plate was the Field's cozy right-field corner?

26. What common feature was "forgotten" in the original plans for this park?

27. To what was Shea Stadium's proposed site adjacent?

28. What years did Shea have co-tenants?

Boxing

1. Whom did Joe Louis defeat by a knockout in round eight to retain his title at Yankee Stadium on June 19, 1946?

2. Who defeated Louis at Yankee Stadium on June 19, 1936?

3. On September 14, 1923, Jack Dempsey got off the canvas to score a second-kayo at the Polo Grounds. Who did Dempsey beat that night?

4. Rocky Marciano's final heavyweight title defense was at Yankee Stadium on September 21, 1955. Who did Marciano stop in nine rounds?

5. Joe Louis' first professional fight in New York City came on June 25, 1935. Louis knocked out a former heavyweight title holder in six rounds. Who did Louis kayo that night?

6. Louis' first title defense in New York went the full 15 rounds, with the champ taking the decision. Who avoided a Louis knockout in the August 30, 1937, fight?

7. Which of the following Joe Louis title defenses did **not** take place in New York City: kayo over Tony Galento; kayo over Johnny Paychek; win by disqualification over Buddy Baer; or kayo over Lou Nova?

8. Whom did Floyd Patterson kayo at the Polo Grounds in his first title defense, July 29, 1957?

9. Name the two great heavyweights who fought twice at Yankee Stadium within a three-month period in 1954.

10. Rocky Marciano fought only one title fight at the Polo Grounds. Whom did he beat there?

11. Who won the first heavyweight title fight ever fought at Yankee Stadium?

12. To whom did Sugar Ray Robinson lose at Yankee Stadium on June 25, 1952?

13. Max Schmeling won the heavyweight crown in a Yankee Stadium bout on June 12, 1930. Whom did Schmeling beat that night to succeed the retired Gene Tunney as champion?

14. Twice within a two-year period the heavyweight title changed hands in bouts fought in Long Island City. Name the fighters in both bouts of the early 1930s.

15. On September 24, 1935, over 88,000 fans packed Yankee Stadium to witness a non-title fight. Who were the fighters?

16. Joe Louis lost only three fights in his pro career, all in New York. One loss was by decision. Who won that fight?

17. Which of the following fights was **not** held at Yankee Stadium?
    (a) The first Sugar Ray Robinson/ Carmen Basilio middleweight title fight
    (b) The first Floyd Patterson/Ingemar Johannson heavyweight title fight
    (c) The second Patterson/Johannson battle
    (d) The Rocky Marciano/Archie Moore heavyweight title battle

18. Within five, can you guess how many heavyweight championship bouts have taken place in New York City?

19. What was the last heavyweight championship bout (as of March 1985)?

20. What was the first heavyweight championship bout in New York City?

21. Who fought for the heavyweight championship most often in New York?

22. He was called the "Jewel of the Ghetto" during his boxing career and became one of the most accomplished referees in the business. Name him.

23. A movie was made of his life story. He held the middleweight champion belt in the '40s and fought Sugar Ray Robinson five times. Who was he?

24. This former light-heavyweight champion went on to be a New York State Athletic

Commission chairman and is also an author. Name him.

25. **Somebody Up There Likes Me** was based on the life story of this New York middleweight champion. Name him.

26. What four title defenses did Ali make in New York?

27. In March 1963 on his way to a title bout, Cassius Clay won a disputed decision in the Garden. Who was the opponent who most ringside observers (except the judges) thought had gotten the better of the fight?

28. What 1962 middleweight title fight at the Garden ended with the tragic death of one of the fighters?

29. What light-heavyweight champion later became an editorial page columnist for **The New York Post**?

30. What New York-born fighter had a chain of pizza joints in the city, and what were they called?

31. What Garden favorite was known for his "bolo punch"?

32. Roberto Duran defeated two brothers in separate fights at the Garden. Who were they?

33. What New York fighter, after losing his championship, sneaked out of Chicago wearing a false beard and mustache?

34. What was Sugar Ray Robinson's real name, and why did he change it?

35. What New York-area heavyweight was the inspiration for **Rocky**?

36. What New York-based champion also designed women's hats?

A Tribute to Madison Square Garden

1. Jack Dempsey fought in Madison Square Garden only once. Who did Dempsey kayo in 12 rounds in December 1920?

2. Yankee Stadium had been called "The House that Ruth Built." What similar name existed for the third Madison Square Garden, situated on Eighth Avenue between 49th and 50th Streets?

3. What was significant about the goal scored by Wilfred "Shorty" Green of the New York Americans on December 15, 1925, against the Montreal Canadiens?

4. Who was selected as the greatest track-and-field performer in Madison Square Garden history in a 1978 poll?

5. In 1958 at the Garden, Seton Hall scored 54 points, while a player on the opposing team totalled 56. Who single-handedly outscored Seton Hall?

6. The first indoor 15-foot pole vault oc-cured in the 1942 Millrose Games at

Madison Square Garden. Who cleared 15 feet?

7. What boxer fought more main events at the Garden than anyone else?

Tennis

1. How many times did Bjorn Borg lose in the finals of the US Open?

2. Whom did McEnroe defeat in the finals to win his first US Open title?

3. Name the two players who have defeated Connors in the finals of the US Open.

4. With whom did Connors team to win the US Open men's doubles championship in 1975, his only Open doubles crown?

5. Name the American doubles team that took the US title in 1968, 1974, 1978 and 1980.

6. How many consecutive US Open singles titles did Chris Evert win in the 1970s?

7. What woman lost four consecutive US Open finals in the 1970s?

8. Through 1985, which of the following players has Chris Evert-Lloyd never

defeated in a US Open final: Pam Shriver, Martina Navratilova, Wendy Turnbull or Hana Mandilkova?

9.   Who was the first player to defeat Evert in a US Open final?

10.   Name the three partners with whom Martina Navratilova has won the US Open doubles crown.

11.   Big Bill Tilden dominated the United States Tennis Championships at Forest Hills in the 1920s, winning the title six straight years. Who was Tilden's great rival, losing the finals to Big Bill five times?

12.   Tilden first reached the finals at Forest Hills in 1918. Who beat Tilden in that year's final match?

13.   Name the Frenchman who snapped Tilden's Forest Hills winning streak by taking the title in 1926.

14.   Name the Frenchman who won the title in 1928.

15.   Which American won back-to-back titles at Forest Hills, in 1931 and 1932?

16.   Which great Englishman won three Forest Hills titles in the 1930s?

17.   Who was the first to win tennis' Grand Slam, completing the feat with a win at Forest Hills?

18.   Name the spunky American who won at Forest Hills in 1939 and 1941, and finished second in 1940.

19. In the nine-year period from 1944 through 1952, four different men won the US title at Forest Hills in two consecutive years. Who won in '44 and '45?

20. Who won in '46 and '47?

21. Won won in '48 and '49?

22. Who won in '51 and '52?

23. Who won in 1950, the only winner of that period who failed to repeat?

24. American Tony Trabert won the US title at Forest Hills in '53 and '55. In between, a fellow American won the crown, his first US championship after two runner-up finishes. Name him.

25. In 1956 this Australian came to Forest Hills with a chance to win the Grand Slam. He reached the finals, but then lost. Name him.

26. Who won that memorable 1956 final match?

27. The great Rod Laver lost in his first Forest Hills final. Name the other Australian left-hander who beat Laver in 1960.

28. In what years did Laver win his two Grand Slams, both climaxed by triumphs at Forest Hills?

29. Name the Mexican who won the US title at Forest Hills in 1963.

30. In what year did the US championship at Forest Hills first become open to professionals?

31. Who won the first US Open?

32. Starting in 1974, eleven straight US Open crowns have been won by left-handers. Jimmy Connors (five titles) and John McEnroe (four titles) have accounted for most of the southpaw wins. Name the other two lefty US champions.

33. Name the American woman who won at Forest Hills seven times between 1923 and 1931.

34. Name the two women (one American, one English) who interrupted her reign as US champion.

35. Who became the queen of Forest Hills in the early 1930s, winning the US crown four straight times (1932-1935)?

36. What American won four titles in five years in the 1936-1940 period, losing only in '37?

37. What Chilean scored the upset win at Forest Hills in 1937?

38. Perhaps best known for her remarkable doubles play, this woman also won the US women's singles crown three straight years, 1948-1950. Name her.

39. Name the darling of the fans who won the women's title three consecutive years. 1951-1953.

40. Two different American women with the same initials won the championship at Forest Hills during the late '50s and early '60s. Name them.

41. What Brazilian woman won three titles at Forest Hills?

42. What woman won at Forest Hills in the first US Open?

43. When did Chris Evert (Lloyd) win her first US Open crown?

44. Name the incredible doubles team that won nine consecutive US titles, and after a four-year lapse came back to win three more in a row.

Horseracing

1. Which of the following horses did not win the Belmont Stakes: Bimelech, High Gun or Tom Fool?

2. Name the jockey who won the Belmont in 1938 and again in 1939.

3. Aboard what horse did Dave Erb win the 1956 Belmont?

4. Willie Saunders won back-to-back Belmont Stakes in 1935 and 1936. Can you name the horses he rode?

5. In 1950 and 1951 the Belmont was won by horses with 12-letter, three-syllable names. Can you name both?

6. Charles Kurtsinger rode Twenty Grand to victory in the 1931 Belmont. What more famous horse did he take to victory in a later Belmont?

7. Which of the following horses did **not** win the Belmont Stakes: Man O'War, Seabiscuit, Johnstown or Native Dancer?

8. Where were the Belmont Stakes run between 1890 and 1905?

9. In what two years were the Belmont Stakes not run?

10. The Belmont was set at a distance of 1½ miles in 1926, and has remained at that length ever since. Which horse won the 1926 1½-mile Belmont Stakes?

11. How many pounds are horses required to carry in the Belmont?

12. Which horse won the Belmont in 1919 to complete the first Triple Crown?

13. There were four Triple Crown winners in the '40s. Name all four.

14. What horse broke the record set at Belmont in 1957?

15. This horse had already won the Kentucky Derby and the Preakness in 1958, when he broke a leg in the homestretch of the Belmont Stakes. He still finished second, but never raced again. Name the horse.

16. Which horse won that ill-fated '58 Belmont?

17. Which horse won the Belmont in 1961, when popular favorite Carry Back failed badly in his attempt to win the Triple Crown?

18. Northern Dancer won the first two legs of the Triple Crown in 1964. Name the horse who won that year's Belmont.

19. When Amberoid won the Belmont Stakes, another Triple Crown bid was foiled. Name the horse Amberoid beat.

20. With what horse did Affirmed battle neck-and-neck to win the Belmont Stakes and Triple Crown in 1978?

21. Which horse spoiled Spectacular Bid's attempt at the Triple Crown in 1979?

22. Which jockey won the Belmont aboard Shut Out, Pavot and One Count?

23. Name the great jockey who won the Belmont aboard Triple Crown winner Gallant Fox in 1930.

24. Which of the following horses was a Belmont Stakes winner: Bold Ruler, Jaipur, Fabius or Candy Spots?

Entertainment

1. What do the movie biographies of Jackie Robinson (Brooklyn Dodgers), Bob Mathias (Millrose Games) and Muhammad Ali have in common?

2. In what movie does a cat become owner of the Brooklyn Dodgers?

3. What country singer and New York Met toured with Loretta Lynn?

4. What was the name of the nightclub Joe Namath had to give up his interest in or face suspension from the NFL?

5. What rhythm-and-blues hit by the Treniers celebrated—and featured the voice—of a great New York athlete?

6. What TV Western star once played first base for the Brooklyn Dodgers?

7. What TV action series star was once a defensive end for the New York Giants?

8. In what move is a triple play pulled off at Shea Stadium?

9. Who played Harlem Globetrotter owner Abe Saperstein in the movie **Go, Man, Go**? (The Trotters played themselves.)

10. What four Rangers made a music video called **The Hockey-Sock Rock**?

11. What hit single featured the voice of Phil Rizzuto?

12. What former Knick became a New York theater producer?

13. Who is the only popular music idol ever to throw out the first ball at Yankee Stadium?

14. In what play have Giant immortal Frank Gifford and his "Monday Night Football" partner Don Meredith co-starred in summer stock around the country?

15. In **Bang the Drum Slowly**, what is the name of the New York baseball team? What about the New York team in **The Natural**?

16. What New York gambler, racketeer and Broadway character is credited with having fixed the 1919 World Series?

17. What former New York Yankees wrote the following autobiographies: (a) **The Bronx Zoo**, (b) **Ball Four** and (c) **Balls**?

18. What New York Knick star of the '70s was also a jazz disc jockey on a local radio station?

19. Who played the Babe Ruth character in **The Natural**, and what was he called in the movie?

20. What was the major difference between the endings of the book and the movie versions of **The Natural**?

21. Name the New York sports figures associated with the following commercial lines:
    (a) "This is _____ for the Money Store."
    (b) "Bonds wants to be your clothing store"
    (c) "Before I make my gorilla dunkies, I get the eaties for my Wheaties."

22. Who played Rocky Graziano in **Somebody Up There Likes Me**?

23. What above-and-beyond-the-call-of-duty course of action was part of Robert de Niro's preparation for playing boxer Jake LaMotta in **Raging Bull**?

24. The Broadway play **The Great White Hope** was based on the life of what prize-fighter?

25. What New York Cosmos star was one of the first celebrities to pose nude for **Playgirl**?

26. What two New York sports figures were the subjects of songs by Bob Dylan?

27. This isn't strictly entertainment, but with what New York business venture were Mickey Mantle and Joe Namath associated?

119

28. Who played Babe Ruth in **Pride of the Yankees**?

29. The US Tennis Open is played in Flushing, Long Island, in a stadium named after not a tennis great, but a music great. Who is this person?

True Miscellany

1. Why did Casey Stengel decide not to give Marvelous Marv Throneberry a cake for his birthday?

2. The 1978-79 Islanders—the team that fell just short of the Stanley Cup they were to gain the following year—had, according to a contemporary newspaper report, only two players who did not practice Transcendental Meditation. Who were they?

3. To what current New York sports figure was Rudyard Kipling's poem "If . . ." dedicated?

4. A New York athlete made headlines for the off-season killing of one of his teammates. Who were the two athletes involved?

5. A New York Ranger of the 1960s had the same name as a NBA player of the '60s, an NFL player of the '60s and a major league baseball player of the '60s. What was his name?

6. What infamous New York killer was the subject of a made-for-TV movie produced by Dave DeBusschere's production company?

7. What ex-New York Ranger was the model for the character played by Paul Newman in **Slap Shot**?

8. What two New York Yankee pitchers swapped wives?

9. A rowdy birthday party for Mickey Mantle at a New York night club led to Billy Martin's being traded away from the Yankees. What was the nightclub?

10. What happened after the Dick Tiger/Frankie DePaula fight at the Garden that made investigators think there might have been a fix?

11. What New York bars are (or were) owned by the following sports figures: (a) Rusty Staub, (b) Phil Linz and (c) Wilt Chamberlain?

12. What job has been held by ex-Met Ron Swoboda, ex-Jet John Docker and ex-Yankee Jim Bouton?

13. What Brooklyn Dodger pitcher, on the eve of the 1955 Dodger/Yankee World Series, said, "I like the Yankees in six"?

14. With whom are the following quotes associated?
    a) "One's a born liar, and the other's convicted."
    b) "I ain't got nothin' against them Viet Congs."
    b) "Come on, Sandy baby, loosen up."

ANSWERS

Baseball

YANKEES

1. Ed Figueroa

2. Graig Nettles

3. Graig Nettles

4. Dick Tidrow

5. Mark Littell

6. Brian Doyle

7. Mike Torrez, who won games three and six

8. Those were the scores by which the Bombers annihilated Boston in the famous four-game sweep at Fenway Park in September of 1978. The sweep moved the Yanks into a tie for first place.

9. Paul Blair

10. Jim Beattie

11. Bill Virdon, Bob Lemon, Clyde King and Yogi Berra

12. .393 by Babe Ruth in 1923

13. Outfielder Earle Combs (1927)

14. Lou Gehrig, with 2,721

15. Gehrig again, with 1,991, 21 more than the Babe. Ruth had 2,204 lifetime RBI's, but not all came while playing for the Yanks.

16. Mel Stottlemyre, with 139

17. Spud Chandler (109-43, for a .717 percentage) and Vic Raschi (120-50 for a .706 mark)

18. Whitey Ford, with 45

19. Ron Guidry and Ed Figueroa

20. Whitey Ford and Jim Bouton

21. Eddie Lopat and Vic Raschi

22. Lefty Gomez and Red Ruffing

23. George Pipgras and Waite Hoyt

24. He yielded Babe Ruth's 60th home run in 1927.

25. Tracy Stallard

26. Charlie Root

27. Lou Gehrig did not play, breaking his streak of 2,130 consecutive games.

28. "Hello there, everybody. This is Mel Allen."

29. Three Ring Pete, the lead character in a series of Ballantine commercials

30. Allie Reynolds, in 1951

31. Bucky Harris

32. Bob Shawkey

33. 1966

34. 1927

35. 1945

36. George "Snuffy" Stirnweiss

37. 1939 (.381) and 1940 (.352)

38. Once. He hit .378 to lead the league in 1924.

39. Once. He hit .363 in 1934.

40. Nick Etten

41. Babe Ruth (1920 and 1921), Lou Gehrig (1927 and a tie for the lead in 1928, and again in 1930 and 1931), and Roger Maris (1960 and 1961)

42. Babe Ruth, with 457 in 1921

43. Mantle hit 52 homers in 1956, and 54 in 1961.

44. Gehrig, with 184 in 1931, the American League record

45. Johnny Mize

46. Jack Chesbro

47. Gehrig, with a .340 mark to DiMaggio's .325

48. Red Ruffing

49. Tommy Henrich

50. Vic Raschi

51. Joe Page

52. Whitey Ford

53. Tom Morgan

54. Gil McDougald

55. Johnny Sain

56. Allie Reynolds

57. Gene Woodling (.306) and Hank Bauer (.304)

58. Eddie Lopat, who won 16 and lost only four

59. Irv Noren

60. Bob Grim

61. Andy Carey

62. Elston Howard

63. Johnny Kucks

64. Tom Sturdivant

65. Bobby Shantz

66. Harry Simpson

67. Hank Bauer, Gil McDougald and good old Harry Simpson

68. Enos Slaughter

69. Bob Turley

70. Hank Bauer

71. Ryne Duren

72. The Chicago White Sox and the Cleveland Indians

73. Bobby Richardson, who batted .301 in '59

74. Sunday

75. Hector Lopez

76. Roger Maris (39 homers, a league-leading 112 RBI's and a .283 batting average)

77. Art Ditmar

78. Bill Skowron

79. Roger Maris (61), Mickey Mantle (54), Bill Skowron (28), Yogi Berra (22), Elston Howard (21) and Johnny Blanchard (21)

80. Elston Howard

81. Bill Stafford

82. Ralph Terry, with a 16-3 record

83. Tom Tresh

84. Frank Lary

85. The Dodgers

86. Joe Pepitone

87. Al Downing started the second game of the Series.

88. Harry Bright

89. Mel Stottlemyre

90. Phil Linz

91. Bobby Richardson

92. The harmonica. He infuriated manager Yogi Berra by playing the harmonica on the team bus after a loss in the heat of a tight pennant race.

93. Allen lost his voice as the Yanks were going down for the fourth straight time to the Dodgers in 1963. Vin Scully had to replace him at the mike.

94. 1960

95. 1964

96. 1961

97. 1954, when the Indians win the flag with an American League record 111 wins

98. 1949

99. 1925

100. 1923

101. Babe Ruth, a three-run shot as the Yanks won 4-1 over Boston

102. 1947

103. The Dawson Award

104. Yogi Berra, in 1947

105. The Braves. While in Milwaukee, they split 14 games with New York in 1957 and 1958.

106. The St. Louis Cardinals beat the Yanks in the 1926, 1942 and 1964 Series, while the Yanks beat St. Louis in 1928 and 1943.

107. Dan Topping and Del Webb

108. 1921

109. 1923

110. Herb Pennock. Pie Traynor broke up the no-hitter with a single.

111. Eddie Stanky

112. Pedro Ramos

113. In 1952 the St. Louis Cardinals re-bounded from an opening game loss to take the Yanks in five. The Yanks got revenge the following year, defeating the Cards in five.

114. 1927 (Pirates) and 1928 (Cubs); 1938 (Cubs) and 1939 (Reds)

115. Bob Turley (21-7 in 1958)

116. Whitey Ford

117. Tony Lazzeri

118. Miller Huggins

119. Ralph Houk

120. Joe Gordon

121. Joe Dugan

122. Frank Crosetti

123. Frank Baker

124. Tom Sturdivant

125. Frank "Spec" Shea

126. Allie Reynolds

127. Vic Raschi

128. Herb Pennock

129. Johnny Murphy

130. Carl Mays (who threw underhanded, or 'submarine' style)

131.   Eddie Lopat

132.   Bob Kuzava

133.   Jim Hunter

134.   Jack Chesbro

135.   George Selkirk

136.   Phil Rizzuto

137.   Bob Turley

138.   Bill Skworon

139.   Hal Chase

140.   Dick Tidrow

141.   Lou Piniella

142.   Ken Brett, Dock Ellis and Willie Randolph

143.   Graig Nettles

144.   Scott McGregor, Tippy Martinez and Rick Dempsey

METS

145.   Frank Thomas

146.   Marvellous Marv Throneberry

147.   Hot Rod Kanehl

148.   They lost their first nine games.

149.   Richie Ashburn hit .306.

150. Bob Miller

151. Robert Lane Miller (a right-hander, 1-12 that year) and Robert Gerald Miller (a southpaw who somehow went 2-2 in 17 appearances)

152. They were 60½ games behind the Giants.

153. Al Jackson, with four. No one else pitched a shutout for the '62 Mets.

154. Carlton Willey

155. Jim Hickman

156. Pete Rose

157. Al Moran

158. Joe Hicks

159. Grover Powell

160. Sherman Jones

161. George Altman

162. Jesse Gonder

163. Charley Smith

164. Joe Christopher hit an even .300.

165. Chris Cannizzaro

166. Roy McMillan

167. Tracy Stallard and Jack Fisher

168. 1965

169. Warren Spahn

170. Dennis Ribant

171. Tom Parsons

172. Gary Kroll

173. Johnny Lewis

174. 1966

175. The Chicago Cubs. Leo Durocher took over the Cubs after their eighth place finish in 1965, and said, "The Cubs are no eighth place ballclub." He turned out to be right, as the Cubs slid to tenth.

176. Ken Boyer

177. Bob Shaw. Dennis Ribant was the other Met with a plus-.500 record, at 11-9 in 1966.

178. Tommy Davis

179. Tom Seaver

180. Jerry Koosman

181. Tommy Agee. Agee hit .271 with 26 homers the following year.

182. Cleon Jones (.340) and Art Shamsky (.300)

183. Ken Boswell

184. Nolan Ryan

185. Five

186. Donn Clendenon

187. Al Weis

188. Jerry Koosman

189. Ron Taylor

190. Gary Gentry

191. J.C. Martin

192. Gary Gentry

193. Tommy Agee

194. Rusty Staub

195. Harry Parker

196. Jon Matlack, a two-hitter in game two

197. George Stone

198. Wayne "Red" Garrett

199. Jerry Koosman and Tug McGraw

200. Yale graduate Ken MacKenzie won five and lost four.

201. Roger Craig, with a 10-24 record

202. Jay Hook

203. Richie Ashburn, with a .306 batting average

204. Second baseman Ron Hunt was chosen as the starting second baseman for the 1964 All-Star Game, played at Shea Stadium. Players were elected by a vote of their peers at the time.

205. John Stephenson

206. Salty Parker

207. Exactly 100

208. None. Felix Millan led the club in batting with a .290 average.

209. Gary Gentry started the third game.

210. Ron Taylor (two innings in the first game loss, and one batter to end game two), Don Cardwell (one inning in the opener) and Nolan Ryan ($2\frac{1}{3}$ innings in game three)

211. Rusty Staub

212. Hobie Landrith

213. Gil Hodges, Charley Neal and Don Zimmer.

214. Felix Mantilla

215. Roger Craig

216. St. Louis (The Mets lost 11-4.)

217. Gus Bell

218. Gil Hodges

219. Jimmy Piersall

220. Pittsburgh (The Pirates beat the Mets 4-3.)

221. Pittsburg (The Pirates again beat the Mets 4-3.)

222. The Chicago Cubs

223. The Houston Astros won ten out of the 12 games played.

224. The expansion of the San Diego Padres

225. Tom Terrific fanned the last ten San Diego hitters.

226. Qualls was the Chicago Cub outfielder whose ninth-inning base hit spoiled Tom Seaver's 1969 bid for a perfect game.

227. Doug Flynn, Pat Zachry, Dan Norman and Steve Handerson

228. Jim Fregosi

229. Amos Otis and Robert Johnson

230. Pitchers Greg Field and Jesse Orosco

231. Ron Darling and Walt Terrell

232. George Stone, with a 12-3 mark

233. John "The Hammer" Milner

DODGERS

234. Dolf Camilli

235. Pete Reiser

236. Kirby Higbe and Whitlow Wyatt

237. Joe Medwick

238. St. Louis, with a 106-48 record

239. Augie Galan

240. McLish

241. Dixie Walker

242. Hal Gregg

243. All tied for first place in the National League, and all lost in a post season play-off.

244. Jackie Robinson and Pee Wee Reese both hit 12 homers to lead the club.

245. Ralph Branca

246. Carl Furillo

247. Hugh Casey

248. Burt Shotton

249. George Shuba

250. Rex Barney

251. Joe Hatten and Jack Banta

252. Cal Abrams

253. Joe Black

254. Russ Meyer

255. Carl Furillo

256. Pee Wee Reese (22), Jim Gilliam (21), Jackie Robinson (17) and Duke Snider (16)

257. Jim Hughes

258. Roger Craig and Don Bessent

259. Sandy Amoros

260. Duke Snider

261. Clem Labine and Roger Craig

262. Ransom Jackson, known as Handsome Ransom, but better known as Randy

263. Carl Erskine and Sal Maglie

264. Clem Labine

265. Jim Gilliam

266. Third

267. Charlie Neal

268. Johnny Podres (2.66) and Don Drysdale (2.69). Warren Spahn actually tied with Drysdale at 2.69.

269. Schaeffer

270. Happy Felton

271. Emmette Kelly

272. Channel 9

273. Jake Daubert (1913 and 1914)

274. Carl Furillo

275. Preacher Roe and Don Newcombe

276. Watson Clark won 20 in 1932, and Luke Hamlin did the same in 1939.

277. Burleigh Grimes

278. Dazzy Vance led from 1922 through 1928.

279. Van Lingle Mungo

280. Fat Freddie Fitzsimmons, at 16-2

281. Dolf Camilli, from 1938 through 1942

282. Jack Fournier, in 1923, 1924 and 1925

283. Jackie Robinson

284. Duke Snider, Roy Campanella and Gil Hodges

285. Boston Red Sox

286. "The Reading Rifle"

287. "Uncle Robbie"

288. "Pistol Pete"

289. "The Little Colonel"

290. "Moonie"

291. Hit four home runs (and a single) against the Boston Braves at Ebbets Field

292. In 1953, with Gil Hodges mired in a terrible batting slump, Father Richmond addressed his congregation one Sunday, saying, "It is too warm this morning for a sermon. Go home, keep the Commandments, and pray for Gil Hodges."

293. The Superbas (or Hanlon's Superbas, after owner/manager Ned Hanlon) and the Robins, after Wilbert Robinson

294. Max Carey

295. Casey Stengel

296. Don Newcombe

297. New York Giant Manager Bill Terry in 1934. The Dodgers knocked Terry's club out of pennant contention by beating the Giants on the last two days of the season.

298. Larry MacPhail

299. Commissioner Happy Chandler suspended Durchoer in 1947.

300. He started the season as manager of the Dodgers and switched over to the Giants in mid-year.

301. Burt Shotton

302. He hooked up with Boston Braves hurler Joe Oeschger, each pitching the entire 26 innings as the Brooks and Braves played to a 1-1 tie. It was the longest game by innings ever played.

303. Dixie Walker

304. Pete Reiser

305. Coombs recorded the first Dodger World Series win in 1916, as the Brooks lost in five games to the Red Sox.

306. Babe Ruth of the Boston Red Sox

GIANTS

307. They are the only Giants in this century to lead the National League in batting average.

308. Johnny Mize (He played for St. Louis before becoming a Giant.)

309. Monte Irvin

310. Carl Hubbell

311. Hoyt Wilhelm (15-3 in 1952)

312. Don Mueller

313. Bill Terry, with 392 (254 hits, 23 homers, 15 triples and 39 doubles, a .401 average)

314. William Voiselle, with 161

315. Johnny Antonelli (20-13 in 1956)

316. Cliff Melton

317. Prince Hal Schumacher

318. Iron Man Joe McGinnity won 31 and 35 in those two years.

319.   1908

320.   Art Nehf

321.   Johnny Antonelli (21-7) and Hoyt
        Wilhelm (12-4)

322.   Larry Benton

323.   Bobby Thompson led the club with 109
        RBI's in 1949, while Hank Thompson
        was team leader with 91 the following
        year.

324.   Alvin Dark, in 1953

325   Travis Jackson

326.   Walker Cooper

327.   Johnny Mize, with 51 homers and 138
        RBI's

328.   Willard Marshall. His next-best season
        for homers was 1953, when he hit 17
        for Cincinnati.

329.   Bill Rigney

330.   George Burns

331.   Ott leads in RBI's-1,860 to 1,859. Willie
        added 44 more RBI's to his career total
        while playing for the Mets.

332.   In 1903, 1919, 1920 and 1921 teams
        were required to win five games to take
        this title.

333.   The great Christy Mathewson blanked
        the Philadelphia Athletics three times in

the 1905 Series. In 27 innings Mathewson allowed only 14 hits, fanned 18, and walked but one batter.

334. 1911 (to the Athletics), 1912 (Red Sox) and 1913 (Athletics)

335. Sal Maglie and Larry Jansen

336. Johnny Antonelli (21-7)

337. Casey Stengel

338. Sal Maglie

339. Eddie Stanky

340. Lefty Gomez

341. Carl Hubbell

342. LeRoy Parmelee

343. John McGraw, as manager of the Giants. He had taken over the club in 1902.

344. Rogers Hornsby

345. Rube Marquard. $11,000 represented his purchase price from Indianapolis.

346. Marquard, in 1912

347. Fred Merkle. "Merkie's Boner" cost the Giants a key game against the Cubs, and probably the pennant as well.

348. Fred Snodgrass, the Giants center fielder

349. Christy Mathewson

350. Fred Lindstrom

351. Jimmy O'Connell

352. Alvin "Cozy" Dolan

353. He recorded 24 consecutive victories, an all-time record.

354. Giant manager John McGraw

355. Monte Irvin

356. "Highpockets"

357. "Blackie"

358. "Prince Hal"

359. "Pep"

360. "The Staten Island Scot"

361. "The Cricket"

362. "The Gause Ghost"

MISCELLANEOUS

363. Ruth, Gehrig, Foxx, Simmons and Cronin

364. Ken Boyer, Stan Musial, Willie Mays and Eddie Mathews

365. Gil Hodges

366. Elston Howard

367. Howard's grounder was fielded by Pee
Wee Reese, who threw to Gil Hodges
for the out.

368. Hugh Casey. Casey entered the game
in the top of the ninth with the bases
loaded and one out. He threw one
pitch, and got Tommy Henrich to hit into an inning-ending double play.

369. Al Gionfriddo and Eddie Miksis

370. Gionfriddo for Carl Furillo, and Miksis
for Pete Reiser, who batted for pitcher
Casey

371. After Furillo walked, Gionfriddo, pinch-
running, stole second. Had he been
thrown out, the game would have ended.

372. With the count on pitch-hitter Reiser
2-and-1, Gionfriddo stole. The pitch
was high for ball three. Yankee manager
Bucky Harris then ordered Reiser, the
potential winning run, to be intentionally
walked.

373. Game five

374. Babe Pinelli. It was his final game
behind the plate.

375. Dale Mitchell

376. Mickey Mantle, in the fourth inning with
two out. He was the first batter on either
team to reach base safely.

377. The Mets. Moock hit .225 in brief duty
in 1967, while Barnes batted .236 in

1972. Barnes batted a lusty .500 for the Mets in '73, with one hit in two at bats.

378. The Dodgers

379. Sal Maglie

380. Don Newcombe

381. Larry Jansen

382. Dodgers 4, Giants 1

383. Alvin Dark

384. Dodger first baseman Gil Hodges was holding the bag against Dark, despite the 4-1 score. He would have fielded Mueller's ball had he not been holding Dark at first.

385. Monte Irvin

386. Whitey Lockman

387. Clint Hartung

388. No balls, one strike

389. Eddie Stanky

390. Rube Walker

391. Willie Mays

392. Noodles Hahn won four and lost two for the Yankees in 1906, and Bubbles batted .278 for the Yanks in 1930.

393. The Dodgers. Bailey (actual name: Abraham Lincoln Bailey) appeared in

seven years of games for the 1921 Dodgers. Walter "Boom-Boom" Beck posted a less-than-glittering 12-20 record for the Bums in 1933, though he hurled 15 complete games, including three shutouts.

394.   The 1917 Giants. Those three started two games a-piece as the Giants lost to the White Sox in six.

395.   Carl Mays and Waite Hoyt, in 1921

396.   Art Nehf

397.   Casey Stengel of the Giants. His homers gave the Giants 5-4 and 1-0 wins in the first and third games of the 1923 Series. Game two that year was played at the Polo Grounds.

398.   Bucky Harris, who played for the Washington Senators during their 1924 Series triumph over the Giants, and managed the Yankees to the World Championship in 1947

399.   Jansen, who won 21 games as a rookie in 1947 and 23 games in 1951. Erskine won 20 games in 1953, his best season.

400.   Newcombe, who won 20 games in 1951 and 1955, and 27 games in 1956. Ford won 25 times in 1961 and 24 times in 1963.

401.   Dusty Rhodes of the Giants, in 1954

402.   Lew Burdette, in 1957

403. Richardson, with 209 hits in 1962

404. The second game of the 1922 Series between the Giants and the Yankees ended in a 3-3 tie after ten innings. The Giants swept the Yanks in the four other games that year.

Football

GIANTS

1. Y.A. Tittle

2. Charlie Connerly

3. Alex Webster

4. 1963. Tittle threw 33 touchdown passes in 1962, a record at the time.

5. Pat Summerall

6. Don Chandler

7. Gary Wood, from Cornell

8. Earl Morrall and Homer Jones, respectively

9. Emlen Tunnell

10. Clarence Childs

11. Erich Barnes

12. Henry Carr

13. Interceptions, with 9

14. Also interceptions: Regan in 1947 with ten, Schnellbacher in 1951 with eleven

15. Dick Lynch

16. Bob Tucker

17. Harry Newman

18. Ed Danowski

19. Tuffy Leemans

20. Bill Paschal (1943 was his rookie season.)

21. Eddie Price

22. Ward Cuff

23. 1963

24. Don Chandler, with 106 points

25. Del Shofner, in 1961

26. Gene Roberts

27. Ron Johnson, in 1970 with 1,027

28. 1959

29. "Choo-Choo," having played college ball at Chattanooga

30. Al DeRogatis

31. Bill Swiacki

32. From the New York Yankees of the AAFC

33. Kyle Rote came to New York in '51, and Frank Gifford followed a year later.

34. 1953. The Giants were 3-9 that year.

35. Ray Wietecha

36. Roosevelt Brown

37. The Rams

38. John Lovetere

39. Don Heinrich and Bob Clatterbuck

40. Harland Svare and Bill Svoboda

41. The Giants beat the Chicago Bears 30-13 in the legendary "sneaker" game to win the NFL title. Trailing 10-3 at half-time, Giant Coach Steve Owen gave his players sneakers for better traction on the icy field. The Giants then routed the previously unbeaten Bears.

42. Ken Strong, now a member of the Pro Football Hall of Fame

43. Jim Lee Howell

44. Frank Gifford and Mel Triplett

45. The Cowboys lost 11 of the 12 games they played in 1960, their first year. They did manage a 31-31 tie with the Giants in a game played at Yankee Stadium.

46. Vince Lombardi

47. Tom Landry

48. The Philadelphia Eagles

49. 1961

50. 1950

51. 1958

52. 1933

53. 1934

54. 1939

55. 1943

56. 1944

57. First in 1946, last in '47; and first again in 1963, last in '64

58. 1966

59. 1963

60. 1966

61. Robert "Cal" Hubbard

62. Frank Filchock

63. Mel Hein

64. Tim Mara

65. Morehead State

66. Allie Sherman

67. Pat Summerall

68. Giant Bob Tucker (1971)

69. Steve Owen

70. Emlen Tunnell

71. Yelberton Abraham

72. Bob Folwell

73. The first sudden death overtime took place.

74. Blitz or "red dog"

75. Chuck Bednarik

76. Jim Thorpe

77. The Giants and the Detroit Lions

78. Henry Carr

79. Pete Gogolak

80. The tuning fork goal post

81. Dave Jennings

82. b) out of 42 attempts

83. Rob Carpenter

84. South Carolina State

85. Bill Arnsparger

86. Joe Danelo, on October 18, 1981

87. c)

88. False. The Giants have three Monday night victories 27-12 over Philadelphia in 1972; 17-14 over Buffalo in 1977; 27-3 over Green Bay in 1983.

89. The Jets, who beat the Giants 26-20 on November 10, 1974, at New Haven

90. Tucker Frederickson

91. Earnest Gray, with 1,139 yards in 1983

92. Louisiana State

93. Missouri

94. Butch Woolfolk from Michigan (1982) and Carl Banks from Michigan State (1984)

95. The Washington Redskins. The Giants beat them 37-13.

JETS

96. The Cleveland Browns

97. Cleveland, 31-21

98. Harry Wismer

99. Sammy Baugh

100. Al Dorow

101. Seven wins and seven losses

102. 1963

103. 1967

104. Larry Grantham

105. 1963

106. Bill Mathis

107. "Wahoo"

108. Cosmo Lacavazzi

109. Gerry Philbin

110. Randy Beverly

111. The Kansas City Chiefs, who topped the Jets 13-6

112. On September 24, Namath passed for 496 yards against the Colts, and on December 11, he passed for 403 yards in a losing cause against the Raiders on "Monday Night Football."

113. Don Maynard with 1,265 yards on 72 catches, and Art Powell with 1,167 on 69

114. Dick Christy

115. Bobby Howfield, with 121 points

116. George Sauer, with 75 catches in 1967

117. Lee Riley, with 11 interceptions

118. Dainard Paulson, with 12

119. Sherman Plunkett

120. Heisman Trophy winner John Huarte of Notre Dame

121. The Oakland Raiders (27-23)

122. Jets 16, Colts 7

123. East Central Oklahoma

124. Steve O'Neal

125. Abdul Salaam

126. George Sauer

127. Weeb Ewbank

128. Jim Turner

129. Jets 32, Oakland 29; Oakland 43, Jets 32

130. Matt Snell

131. Chris Ward

132. Don Maynard

133. John Riggins

134. b)

135. Bob Crable

136. Jerome Barkum

137. Mike Holovak

138. Ken Shipp

139.   Temple

140.   They beat the Vikings 14-7.

141.   Never

142.   John Riggins, with 1,005 in 1975

143.   Freeman McNeil, with 736 yards in the strike-shortened 1982 season

144.   They are the only teams with perfect records in Super Bowl appearances. The Steelers have four victories, the Packers and 49ers have two apiece while the Jets have their great win in Super Bowl III.

145.   Perhaps not suprisingly, the Jets have lost all three times they have played the Dallas Cowboys. They are also 0-3 against the Washington Redskins. More amazingly, the Jets are also 0-3 against the Philadelphia Eagles.

146.   Clark Gaines

147.   Mickey Shuler, with 68

COLUMBIA

148.   1961

149.   Harvard

150.   Princeton, by a 30-20 score. The Lions beat Harvard 26-14.

151.   Tom Vassell

152. Aldo "Buff" Donelli

153. Lou Gehrig

154. Bill Campbell

155. 1947

156. Gene Rossides

157. Bill Swiacki

158. 21-20

159. The reference was to NYU, after a controversy erupted over the outcome of the 1922 football game between the two schools. Both teams claimed (and still claim) victory.

160. Webb '10, Watkins '24, and Ford '23 wrote "Roar, Lion Roar." The song was awarded first prize at the Columbia Alumni Federation song contest of 1923.

Basketball

KNICKS

1. Dave DeBusschere, Bill Bradley, Willis Reed, Walt Frazier and Dick Barnett

2. Dave DeBusschere

3. His photographic memory (He memorized the Manhattan phone book, etc.)

4. Dave Stallworth and Mike Riordan

5. Danny Whelan

6. Milwaukee Bucks

7. Bernard King, with 60 points

8. Richie Guerin, with 57 points

9. Bill Cartwright

10. Ernie Grunfeld

11. John Gianelli

12. Walt Frazier

13. Fort Hamilton, Brooklyn

14. CCNY

15. Dick McGuire

16. Nate Bowman

17. Walt Frazier and Earl Monroe

18. Andrew "Fuzzy" Levane

19. Ken Sears

20. The Syracuse Nationals, 2-0

21. Emmette Bryant

22. Bud Palmer

23. Vince Boryla

24. The Minneapolis Lakers beat New York in the final round 4-1.

25. Ernie Vandeweghe

26. Jumpin' Honny Green

27. Dick Garmaker

28. Darrall Imhoff

29. Dave Budd, Cleveland Buckner, Al Butler and Donnis Butcher (In '62 they also briefly had Ed Burton on the roster.)

30. Gene Shue

31. Tom Gola

32. Gene Conley

33. Sam Stith ('61-'62) and Tom Stith ('62-'63)

34. Jack Foley

35. Paul Hogue

36. Len Chappell

37. Barry Kramer

38. Jim "Bad News" Barnes

39. Howard Komives

40. The Celtics won four of seven against New York, and the Hawks won four out of six.

41. Fewest points allowed. The Knicks yielded 8,682, with the Lakers next best at 9,164. The Knicks were next to last in the league in rebounds.

42. Walt Frazier with a .518 mark

43. Cazzie Russell

44. Nate Bowman

45. Five. The Lakers took game one, the Knicks won the next four.

46. Second place in the Atlantic Division, 11 games behind Boston. The Knicks topped the Celtics in seven games in the Eastern Conference Finals.

47. As in '69-'70, the Knicks led in fewest points allowed, 8,053 for a per-game average of 98.2.

48. Jerry Lucas, with a .513 mark. Actually Dean Meminger had a .515 average, but the Dream did not have enough attempts to qualify for the official listing of league leaders.

49. Henry Bibby

50. Neil Cohalan

51. Harry Gallatin in '53-'54

52. Carl Braun

53. Nat "Sweetwater" Clifton

54. The Baltimore Bullets (4-3), and the Milwaukee Bucks (4-1)

55. Jerry Lucas, replacing the injured Willis Reed

56. Walt Bellamy and Howard Komives

57. The Rochester Royals

58. Willis Reed, in 1965

59. They were all on the roster of the 1970 championship Knick team.

60. Dick and Al McGuire

61. Bill Bradley

62. Walt Frazier

63. Earl Monroe

64. Bradley scored 1,319 points in the '72-'73 season, while Braun's top total

was 1,173 in '57-'58. Braun averaged 16.5 ppg that year, however, to Bradley's mark of 16.1.

65. Reed's top mark was 1,755 points, while Naulls' went over 1,800 points. twice, with a high of 1,877 in '61-'62, when he averaged 25.0 ppg.

66. Sears, who averaged 21.0 in '58-'59. DeBusschere never reached the 20-point plateau.

67. McGuire

68. The same as the all-time record: 100 by Wilt Chamberlain

69. Tom McMillen and Jim McMillian, acquired in separate trades with the Buffalo Braves

70. Ernie "Doc" Vandeweghe

71. 19

72. "The Horse"

73. "Butch"

74. "Trooper"

75. Big Cat

76. Dayton

77. Providence

78. Wichita State

79. Southern Illinois

80. Tennessee State

81. St. Johns

82. Wichita State

83. North Dakota

84. Grambling

85. Ohio State

86. Detroit University

87. Princeton

88. Michigan

NETS

89. Long Island Arena, in Commack, Long Island

90. The Virginia Squires. Just like Dr. J., Barry never played for the Squires—he played for the ABA Washington Capitals. The franchise was transferred to Virginia, and Barry was sold to the Nets before the season started.

91. He was ordered by a judge to honor his previous contract with the Golden State Warriors of the NBA.

92. Billy Paultz

93. Dave DeBusschere

94. He was the player traded (along with a big bunch of cash) to Virginia for Dr. J.

95. University of Massachusetts

96. 1976

97. Roy Boe, then owner of the Nets

98. It's estimated at $3 million.

99. Art Heyman if you count the New Jersey Americans; Tom Hoover if you don't.

100. Albert King

101. Michael Ray Richardson and Ray Williams

102. Not to get into the NBA—they'd already paid big bucks for that—but to get the permission to move to New Jersey

103. Kevin Loughery

104. Rod Thorn

105. Piscataway

106. Jan von Breda Kolff

107. Willie Sojourner

108. Bill Melchionni

109. Dr. J. and Tiny A

110. Darryl Dawkins

111. Wendell Ladner

112. Max Zaslofsky

113. Walt Simon

Hockey

RANGERS

1. The New York Americans

2. Billy Burch, with 22 goals and three assists

3. The Chicago Black Hawks and the Detroit Cougars (later the Falcons, and then the Red Wings)

4. First place, with a 25-13-6 record

5. Three

6. 1940

7. Toronto

8. Six

9. Frank Boucher

10. 1928 and 1933

11. Lester Patrick

12. None

13. Andy Bathgate

14. Chuck Rayner

15. "Buddy" O'Connor

16. Frank Boucher

17. Edgar Laprade

18. Andy Hebenton ('57) and Camille Henry ('58)

19. Jean Ratelle

20. Gilles Villemure

21. Dave Kerr, in '39-'40

22. Roy Worters of the Americans in '30-'31

23. Dave Schriner of the Americans

24. Grant Warwick

25. Lorne Worsley and Camille Henry

26. Steve Vickers

27. Doug Harvey, the former Montreal great, in '62

28. Harry Howell, in 1967

29. The Calder Trophy, in 1949

30. Alf Pike

31. Doug Harvey

32. George "Red" Sullivan

33. Lester Patrick

34. Bill Cook

35. Earl Seibert

36. Cecil Dillon of the Rangers and Gordon Drillon of the Leafs

37. Right wing

38. Defenseman Bill Gadsby

39. Dan Raleigh

40. Wally Hergeshimer

41. Danny Lewicki

42. Marcel Paille

43. Bryan Hextall

44. Lynn Patrick. Hextall scored 24, and led the club and league in scoring with 56 points to Patrick's 54.

45. Andy Bathgate

46. Bill Gadsby

47. Doug Harvey. Harvey had previously won the award six times as a member of the great Montreal Canadiens.

48. Harry Howell

49. Camille Henry

50. Jim Neilson

51. "Gump," "The Cat," "Leapin' Looie" and "Bones"

52. Jim Neilson

53. Rod Gilbert

54. 1940

55. Frank Boucher

56. Ka-CHOOK; TAY-chuck

57. Doug Harvey

58. Rod Gilbert, Jean Ratelle and Vic Hadfield

59. "Goal-a-game"

60. Nick Fotiu

61. A broken back

62. Jacques Plante

63. Ed Giacomin

64. Jean Ratelle, Brad Park, Rick Middleton and Joe Zanussi

65. Ken Hodge

66. He had been an NHL referee.

67. "I'd rather see the Rangers show a profit at the bottom line than win the Stanley Cup."

68. Frank Boucher

69. Leading the league in penalty minutes for a season

70. "Storey is a bum!"

71. Mike Bossy

72. John Ferguson

73. From the Winnipeg Jets of the World Hockey Association

74. Bobby Hull

75. Ron Greschner

76. The US Olympic gold medal winners

77. Gilles Villemure

78. Andy Bathgate

79. Bryan Hextall

80. George Leone

81. Ed Giacomin and Gilles Villemure

82. Steve Vickers

83. Terry Sawchuck

84. Lester Patrick

85. "The Fog"

86. Mark Pavelich

87. They went over the 100-point mark, with 109, 109 and 102 in those three years.

88. b) The Rangers won 49 games in '70-71.

89. The Rangers sent Mike McEwen, Pat Hickey, Lucien DeBlois and Dean Turner to Colorado, plus "future considerations," which turned out to be Bobby Crawford.

90. Ron Greschner

91. Anders Hedberg

92. Dave. He was born on July 31, 1956; Don was born September 5, 1958.

93. Pierre Larouche

ISLANDERS

94. Phil Goyette

95. 12

96. Ken Morrow

97. Clark Gillies

98. Denis Potvin

99. Both of them

100. Mike Bossy

101. Bob Nystrom

102. John Tonelli and Lorne Henning

103. Rocky

104. Brent and Duane

105. Ed Westfall and Jean Potvin

106. The Colorado Rockies

107. Lorne Henning

108. St. Louis

109. Bobby Nystrom

110. Eddie Westfall

111. Denis Potvin

112. Phil Goyette

113. Earl Ingarfield

114. Clark Gilles

115. Billy Harris and Dave Lewis

116. "Trio Grande"

117. Lorne Henning, Gary Howatt, Bobby Nystrom and Billy Smith

118. Bryan Trottier

119. Denis Potvin

120. J.P. Parise

121. **Power On Ice**

122. Wayne Merrick

123. Cantiague Park

124. Mike Kaszycki

125. "Radar"

126. "Dog"

127. "Pup"

128. "Rat"

129. "The Hammer of Thor"

130. "Bam-Bam"

131. Eddie Westfall

Photos

1. 26th Street and Madison Avenue

2. A roof

3. 1890

4. Stanford White

5. Eighth Avenue between 49th and 50th Streets

6. A six-day bike race

7. February 11, 1968

8. Seventh and Eighth Avenues and 31st and 33rd Streets

9. Polo Grounds (September 29, 1880)

10. The Boston Red Sox (May 1, 1881)

11. Manhattan Field

12. Harlem River

13. Horseshoe or bathtub like

14. The Mets lost to Philadelphia 5-1, September 18, 1964.

15. The Polo Grounds

16. The Red Sox, April 18, 1923. The Yankees won 4-1 on a Babe Ruth three-run homer.

17. "Death Valley"

18. Babe Ruth, Lou Gehrig, manager Miller Huggins and club president Edward Barrow

19. A lumber yard

20. 1976

21. Sullivan Place (first base), McKeever Place (third base), Montgomery Street (left field) and Bedford Avenue (right field)

22. September 24, 1957. The Dodgers beat Pittsburg 3-0.

23. "Dodger Sym-phonie"

24. Team president Charles Ebbets

25. 301 feet

26. A press box

27. The home of the New York World's Fairs (1939-40 and 1964)

28. The Mets and the Yankees shared Shea in 1974-75.

Boxing

1. Billy Conn

2. Max Schmeling

3. Luis Firpo

4. Archie Moore

5. Primo Carnera

6. Tommy Farr

7. The Buddy Baer fight, which took place in Washington, D.C.

8. Tommy "Hurricane" Jackson

9. Rocky Marciano and Ezzard Charles. Marciano won in a decision on June 17, and by kayo in round eight on September 17.

10. Roland LaStarza, an 11th-round kayo on September 24, 1953

11. Gene Tunney. He kayoed Tom Heeney in 11 rounds on July 21, 1928.

12. Joey Maxim

13. Jack Sharkey

14. Jack Sharkey defeated Max Schmeling on June 21, 1932, at Long Island City, and Max Baer kayoed Primo Carnea there on June 14, 1934.

15. Joe Louis and Max Baer (Louis kayoed Baer in four rounds.)

16. Ezzard Charles, on September 27, 1950

17. (c) It was held at the Polo Grounds.

18. Forty-three

19. Larry Homes by a 12th-round kayo over Mike Weaver

20. James Jeffries over Bob Fitzsimmons, a kayo in the 11th round. The fight took place at Coney Island in 1899.

21. Joe Louis (19 times)

22. Ruby Goldstein

23. Jake LaMotta

24. Jose Torres

25. Rocky Graziano

26. Floyd Patterson, Zora Folley, Ken Norton and Earnie Shavers (not Joe Frazier—the Ali/Frazier fight at the Garden was Frazier's title defense)

27. Doug Jones

28. Emile Griffith/Benny "Kid" Paret

29. Jose Torres

30. Rocky Graziano; Rocky Graziano's Pizza Ring

31. Kid Gavilan

32. Edwin and Alfonzo Viruet

33. Floyd Patterson

34. Walker Smith; he needed a fake ID when he entered the Golden Gloves because he was too young.

35. Chuck Wepner

36. Emile Griffith

A Tribute to Madison Square Garden

1. Bill Brennan

2. "The House that Tex Built," after Tex Rickard, president, general manager, and prime boxing promoter of the Garden

3. It was the first goal scored in the Eighth Avenue Garden.

4. Glenn Cunningham

5. Oscar Robertson of Cincinnati

6. Cornelius Warmerdam

7. Beau Jack (21)

Tennis

1. Four. In 1976 and 1978 Borg lost to Jimmy Connors, and in 1980 and 1981 he lost to John McEnroe.

2. Vitas Gerulaitis, in 1979

3. Manuel Orantes in 1975, and Guillermo Vilas in 1977

4. Ilie Nastase

5. Stan Smith and Bob Lutz

6. Four (1975-1978)

7. Evonne Goolagong (1973-1976)

8. Navratilova

9. Tracy Austin, in 1979

10. Betty Stove (1977), Billie Jean King (1978 and 1980) and Pam Shriver (1983 and 1984)

11. "Little Bill" Johnston

12. R. Lindley Murray

13. Rene Lacoste, who repeated in '27, topping Tilden in the final

14. Henri Cochet

15. Ellsworth Vines

16. Fred Perry (in '33, '34 and '36)

17. Don Budge

18. Bobby Riggs

19. Frank Parker

20. Jack Kramer

21. Pancho Gonzales

22. Australian Frank Sedgman

23. Art Larsen

24. Vic Seixas

25. Lew Hoad

26. Ken Rosewall

27. Neale Fraser

28. 1962 and 1969

29. Rafael Osuna

30. 1968

31. Arthur Ashe

32. Spaniard Manuel Orantes (1975) and Argentinian Guillermo Vilas (1977)

33. Helen Wills Moody (She won the first six as Helen Wills.)

34. American Molla Mallory won in 1926, and England's Betty Nuthall won in 1930.

35. Helen Jacobs

36. Alice Marble

37. Anita Lizana

38. Margaret Osborne du Pont

39. Maureen "Little Mo" Connolly

40. Doris Hart ('54 and '55) and Darlene Hard ('60 and '61)

41. Maria Bueno

42. Virginia Wade

43. 1975

44. Louise Brough and Margaret Osborne (du Pont) won from 1942 through 1950, and again in '55, '56 and '57.

Horseracing

1. Tom Fool

2. James Stout, aboard Pasteurized and Johnstown

3. Needles

4. Omaha and Granville

5. Middleground in 1940, and Counterpoint in 1951

6. War Admiral, in 1937

7. Seabiscuit

8. Morris Park

9. 1911 and 1912

10. Crusader

11. 126

12. Sir Barton

13. Whirlaway ('41), Count Fleet ('43), Assault ('46) and Citation ('48)

14. Secretariat, in 1973.

15. Tim Tam

16. Cavan

17. Sherluck

18. Quadrangle

19. Kauai King, in 1966

20. Alydar

21. Coastal

22. Eddie Arcaro, who also won with Whirlaway, Citation and Nashua

23. Earl Sande

24. Jaipur, in 1962

Entertainment

1. Robinson, Mathias and Ali all played themselves

2. **Rhubarb**

3. Doug Flynn

4. Bachelors III

5. "Say-Hey (The Willie Mays Song)"

6. Chuck Connors ("The Rifleman")

7. Fred Dryer ("Hunter")

8. **The Odd Couple**

9. Dane Clark

10. Phil Esposito, Ron Duguay, Anders Hedberg and Pat Hickey

11. "Paradise by the Dashboard Light," by Meat Loaf

12. Earl Monroe

191

13. Paul Simon

14. **The Odd Couple**

15. The Mammoths; the Knights

16. Arnold Rothstein

17. (a) Sparky Lyle, (b) Jim Bouton and (c) Graig Nettles

18. Spencer Haywood

19. Joe Don Baker; "The Whammer"

20. In the book, the character strikes out to throw the last game of the World Series; in the movie he hits a home run to win it.

21. (a) Phil Rizzuto, (b) Joe Torre and (c) Darryl Dawkins

22. Paul Newman

23. He gained sixty pounds.

24. Jack Johnson

25. Shep Messing

26. Catfish Hunter and Ruben "Hurricane" Carter

27. An employment agency—Mantle Men and Namath Girls

28. He played himself.

29. Louis Armstrong

True Miscellany

1. As Stengel put it, "We were afraid he'd drop it."

2. Ed Westfall and Billy Smith

3. Mets president Nelson Doubleday, then the infant son of Kipling's publisher

4. Terry Sawchuk of the Rangers was killed by a teammate Ron Stewart, who pushed him down during a family barbecue. The incident was ruled an accident. Stewart later went on to coach the Rangers.

5. Larry Brown

6. "Son of Sam," or David Berkowitz

7. Reggie Fleming

8. Fritz Peterson and Mike Kekich

9. The Copacabana

10. After being knocked out with barely a glove laid on him, DePaula went to a New York night club, where he an-

nounced loudly, "We really made a killing tonight!"

11. (a) Rusty's, (b) Mr. Laff's, and (c) Small's Paradise (known when Wilt owned it as Wilt Chamberlain's Small Paradise)

12. Sportscasters for New York TV stations

13. Billy Loes

14. a) Billy Martin
    b) Muhammad Ali
    c) Ex-Jet John Riggins

Irv Finkel grew up on Gerard Avenue in the Bronx, where his bedroom window directly faced Yankee Stadium. From the roof of his building, he watched the classic 1958 football championship game between the Giants and the Colts. His own sports career includes organizing and playing third base for the Doughboys, who won the 1979 East Coast Challenge Cup for softball. Currently, Finkel serves as sports editor for **The Woodstock Times**.

During his senior year at Columbia University, **Douglas Grunther** captained the varsity tennis team to its first-ever Ivy League championship. He is the producer and host of WDST-FM's "Conversations" in Woodstock, New York, and of "Flashback," a live trivia show which he performs at resorts, colleges, clubs and corporate events. Grunther has been called "the number-one host of live trivia events in the East" by **The New Yorker**.